D1162452

A Garland Series

The English Stage
Attack and Defense 1577 - 1730

A collection of 90 important works
reprinted in photo-facsimile in 50 volumes

edited by
Arthur Freeman
Boston University

Serious Reflections
on the Scandalous Abuse and Effects of the Stage

A Second Advertisement Concerning the Profaneness of the Play-House

A Sermon Preached in the Parish-Church of St. Butolph's Aldgate

by

Arthur Bedford

with a preface
for the Garland Edition by

Arthur Freeman

Garland Publishing, Inc., New York & London

1974

Library of Congress Cataloging in Publication Data

Bedford, Arthur, 1668-1745.
  Serious reflections on the scandalous abuse and
effects of the stage.

  Reprint of 3 works: the 1st printed in 1705, by W.
Bonny, Bristol; the 2d printed in 1705; the 3d printed in
1730, by C. Ackers, London.
  1. Theater--Moral and religious aspects. 2. Thea-
ter--England--History--Sources. 3. Church of England--
Sermons. 4. Sermons, English. I. Bedford, Arthur,
1668-1745. A second advertisement concerning the
profaneness of the play-house. 1974. II. Bedford,
Arthur, 1668-1745. A sermon preached in the parish-
church of St. Butolph's Aldgate. 1974. III. Title.
IV. Title: A second advertisement concerning the profaneness of the play-house. V. Title: A sermon
preached in the parish-church of St. Butolph's Aldgate.
PN2047.B49   1974   792'.013   78-170475
ISBN 0-8240-0624-0

Preface

Arthur Bedford was born at Tiddenham or Tidenham, near Cheapstowe, Gloucestershire, some twenty-five miles from Bristol, in 1668, and went up to Brasenose College, Oxford, where he graduated B.A. in 1687/8 and proceeded M.A. in 1691. Ordained in 1688, he returned to his county and served as vicar of Temple-Church, Bristol, from 1692 to 1713. With the commotion initiated by Jeremy Collier's Short View *(1698) and its predictable replies, Bedford threw himself into the fray, at first with a relatively modest sermon preached 7 January 1705 at Temple-Church. Published as* Serious Reflections on the Scandalous Abuse and Effects of the Stage *by the congenial London printer William Bonny, now transplanted to Bristol and by 1703 "stark blind" (John Dunton), Bedford's sermon may have brought him to the attention of Wriothesley, Duke of Bedford, whose chaplain he became in the following year. It was occasioned, he says, by "the Acting of* Comedies *and* Tragedies *in* St. James's *Parish during the time of the Fair in the year 1704" and the actual building of "a* Play-house *in the City of* Bath, *and the great Apprehensions that such a Design was carried on this city [Bristol]."*

5

PREFACE

Inter alia, *the portent of a tempest which alarmed many in 1703 is evoked to warn citizens of Bristol of the course matters were taking. Bonny's advertisements comprise only attacks on the stage.*

But by 23 July 1705 a theatrical manager, Mr. Power, and his troupe had established a semi-permanent playhouse at Bristol, and had staged Love for Love *in defiance of Collier's extreme strictures and the antagonism alike of local authorities and clergy. One non-clerical opponent published a* Concio Laici *or Layman's Sermon, taking up cudgels where the Church had evidently left them (Bedford,* Evil and Danger, *pp. 12 ff.), but no copy of this attack has come to light. Conceivably it is the same "advertisement" cited as "lately shewn" in* Serious Reflections, *and printed to discourage further stage-playing. Subsequently there appeared* A Second Advertisement *concerning the Profaneness of the Play-House, of which only* B^8 *(16 pages, surely lacking the preliminaries) survives in the British Museum, and which is unreasonably attributed to Bedford by* BMC *and by Lowe. Its title implies a connection with the lost* Concio Laici, *and its tone is more obviously secular than Bedford's; nor is it mentioned in the advertisements to* Evil and Danger *(1706) which do include* Serious Reflections *and a prior essay on the misuse of sacred music in popular domain. We do reprint the text of* A Second Advertisement, *but offer no claim for Bedford's authorship.*

PREFACE

The first of Bedford's two major assaults on the stage, The Evil and Danger of Stage-Plays, *appeared in the following year, once more printed by Bonny at Bristol, but now on sale, by Henry Mortlake, at London. A kind of sequel of Collier's* Short View *("Immorality and Profaneness": "Evil and Danger"), it claims to include "almost Two Thousand* Instances, *taken from the* Plays *of the two last Years, against all the* Methods *lately used for their* Reformation." *Treating briefly of the events at Bristol, account is given of Mr. Power's first playing of* Love for Love *(23 July 1705), as well as of* The Provok'd Wife *(13 August following), for which the company were sternly admonished and fined, and a temporary end to professional theatre in that city effected.*

Reverend Bedford obtained the living of Newton St. Loe, Somersetshire, in 1713, and probably remained there as rector some eleven years, although he did not resign tne place until 1737. In 1719 he offered to the world a treatise on the literal immorality of the drama which is exceeded for scholastic and precisionist zeal not even by its spiritual forefather Histriomastix. A Serious Remonstrance in behalf of the Christian Religion . . . against . . . English Play-Houses — *now printed, as Lowe-Arnott-Robinson omit to mention, at London, by John Darby, for booksellers in Bath, Bristol, and Oxford — cites "almost Seven Thousand Instances [of profaneness and im-*

7

PREFACE

morality] taken out of the Plays of the present Century, and especially of the five last Years," along with *"above Fourteen Hundred Texts of Scripture, which are mentioned in this Treatise, either as ridicul'd and expos'd by the Stage, or as opposite to their present Practices,"* the latter catalogued in sixteen double-columned pages. Virtually unique of its kind, this exhaustive compendium speaks a long and desperately thorough immersion in the tainted literature (although as usual there is no indication of actual theater-going), and may stand as a high-water mark of pietistic/diabolist anti-theatrical paranoia. In Evil and Danger we learned that "God" is pronounced 23 times in The Duchess of Malfi; here we are confronted with the "wickedness" of even mock-sorcery, the "blasphemy" of Macbeth, and the unforgivable attribution to human agency of such heavenly action or forbearance as love, luck, and safety. The extent of Bedford's imagination in identifying transgression is astounding: "When correctly viewed," as Mr. Lehrer puts it, latterly, "everything is lewd."*

In 1724 Bedford came to live at Hoxam, and subsequently held the post of Lecturer of St. Botolph's, Aldersgate. In this capacity he preached a sermon on 29 November 1729, "occasioned by the erecting of a play-house in the neighborhood," printed (1730) by Charles Akers for J. Hooke, W. Meadows, and T. Cox. "The Erecting of a Play-

8

PREFACE

House *in the Neighbourhood obliges me to warn this Congregation of the great Evil and Danger in Frequenting them,"* he explains, *but full twenty-five years after his similar preachment at Bristol, Bedford was not above putting his rhetoric to second use. With a few minimal rephrasings and omissions of local or timebound allusions, and a few updatings (notably a longish attack, pp. 22-5, on* The Beggar's Opera*) the new sermon is the old sermon* verbatim. *In an appendix Bedford cites as "unanswered" his larger works of 1706 and 1719. A "second edition" (for John Wilford, the pamphlet specialist, 1735; not in Lowe-Arnott-Robinson, British Museum 1112.e.18[1]) is no more than the 1730 sheets with a cancel title.*

*The lucrative new playhouse in Goodman's Fields, opened by Thomas Odell 31 October 1729, was ordered closed on 28 April 1730 "because of the complaints of the Lord Mayor and Aldermen" (Nicholl, II, 284), but "under circumstances which are not clear, Odell commenced production again on 11 May and continued playing until the end of the regular season" (*London Stage, *III, xxii; cf.* MLN, *XXV [1930], 443-56). Garrick made his first London appearance here in 1741, and the playhouse was still in operation in 1742. It was demolished in 1746.*

Arthur Bedford is treated briefly by DNB, *slightly by* CBEL, *less by* NCBEL, *and summarily by Foster,* Alumni Oxoniensis, *and Nichols,* Illus-

trations. *Joseph Wood Krutch,* Comedy and Conscience after the Restoration *(rev. ed., New York,
1949) terms him "an industrious pedant," although Defoe "read him with approval." He was
no narrow scholar: he wrote two books intelli-
gently disputing Sir Isaac Newton's* Ancient
Chronology, *made a mark as an orientalist, a critic
of modern music, and an astronomer. Late in life
he attended Frederick, Prince of Wales, as chaplain,
and from 1724 onward was chaplain as well of
Ashe's Hospital in Hoxam, where he took up his
final residence and died (13 August 1745), aged
78, from the effects of making outdoor observations on the comet of that year.*

Serious Reflections *is reprinted from a copy at
Yale (Beinecke Hag 12 2 v.2). It collates A-1⁴ (72
pp.), with vertical chainlines.* A Second Advertisement *is reprinted from British Museum 641.e.16
(3), collating B^8, with vertical chainlines. It is
mostly uncut at the foot, but all leaves are
guarded, slightly affecting a few inner margins.
Although Lowe-Arnott-Robinson do not evidently
regard this copy as imperfect, it seems almost
certainly to lack preliminaries; but I know of no
other copy.* The Evil and Danger of Stage-Plays *is
reprinted from the Yale copy (Beinecke Haf 21
706b) collating $A^7 B\text{-}P^8 Q^4$. In this text $B1^r$ exists
in two states, one (cancelled) bearing the inflam-
matory title "Hell upon Earth, or, the Language of
the Play-House," which we print as an appendix*

PREFACE

from Lowe's copy, now at Harvard (Thr.417.06*).
It should be noted that neither of the British
Museum copies contains this leaf, as Lowe-Arnott-
Robinson suggest. A Serious Remonstrance *is re-*
printed from a copy at Yale (Beinecke Haf 21
7196) collating $A^4 a^4 b^2 B$-$Z^8 Aa$-Bb^8 *(440 pp.,*
vertical chainlines). A Sermon, *1730, is reprinted*
from British Museum 225.h.11 (2.), collating π^1
A-E^4 (42 pp., vertical chainlines), compared with
Harvard Thr. 417.30*.

April, 1972   A.F.

SERIOUS
Reflections

On the Scandalous
Abuse and Effects

OF THE
STAGE:
IN A
SERMON

Preach'd at the Parish-Church
of *St. Nicolas* in the City of
Bristol, on *Sunday* the 7th
Day of *January,* 170$\frac{4}{5}$.

By ARTHUR BEDFORD, M. A.
Vicar of *Temple-Church* in the
aforesaid City.

BRISTOL,
Printed and sold by *W. Bonny* in *Corn-street,* 1705

THE
PREFACE
TO THE
READER

THE following Sermon was preached at *S. Nicolas's* Church in the City of *Bristol*, being occasioned by the Acting of *Comedies* and *Tragedies* in St. *James's* Parish during the time of the Fair in the Year 1704. the actual building of a *Play-house* in the City of *Bath*, and the great Apprehensions that such a Design was carried on in this City. Accordingly I thought it my Duty to prevent (as far as lay in me) the sad Effects thereof, to disswade such as then heard me, from the frequenting the

same

same, with the most proper Arguments I could think of, and also to awaken their Consciences (if possibly I could) with the sense of God's Judgments inflicted on us for our Sins, and (as I fear) for this Particular. But the Misrepresentations of this Sermon (by some who heard it, and others who heard of it) have obliged me to publish the same, that such as have conceived a Prejudice against it, may upon a serious Perusal be better Judges of those particular Expressions which have fallen under the Censure of some Men, whether they deserve that heavy. Load which hath been cast upon them. However, as I have reason to hope that the Preaching thereof had its desired Effect in some measure at that Time; so, if the Printing may farther contribute to the same End, I shall be thankful to God for those Scandals and Aspersions which made it so necessary. Indeed as it was composed in the time of the Holy-days, when there were more than usual

Avocations

Avocations from Study, and Diſtraction of Thoughts; and as it was calculated for the Capacity of the Meaneſt, ſo the Reader muſt not expeƈt a polite and well-fram'd Diſcourſe, eſpecially ſince I think that the making any Amend-ments in ſuch Expreſſions which were expoſed to Cenſure, or the leaving out of any Particular, would be an Impoſi-tion upon him. For my own Part, I have ſincerely aimed only at the Glory of God and the Publick Good of the City wherein I live, and am therefore the better ſatisfied in undergoing evil, as well as good Report, eſpecially when I conſider that ſuch who were much better than my ſelf (even the Apoſtles of *Chriſt*) did *rejoyce when they were accounted worthy to ſuffer Shame for his ſake.* There is no Man who deſires to be leſs concerned in Popular Quarrels than my ſelf; and therefore I ſhould have been glad could I be free from them upon any Terms except the Negleƈt of my Duty in for-

bearing

The Preface.

Isai. 58. 1. bearing to reprove the Vices of the Age. For this Reason I shall take no Notice of any Personal Censures or Reflections, but only endeavour to wipe off such which relate to the Subject of the following Discourse.

Sect. 7 and 8. First, Some have been offended because *I was too particular in describing the Judgments of God, which have lately befallen this Nation, and imputed the same to the Abominations of the Play-house.* I think the Reasons which I offered were sufficient for such a Conjecture; and therefore if People will not take Warning by such Alarms, they are guilty of the greater Provocation; and indeed, if such Judgments will not reclaim us, God may justly suffer us to go on without Correction for the future, and fill up the Number of our Iniquities until Vengeance come upon us to the uttermost. When our *Gracious Queen* was pleased to issue out her *Royal Proclamation*

mation for a *General Fast*, occasioned by the late *Storm* and *Tempest*, it is very remarkable that most of our *Right Reverend Bishops* and the *Clergy* in the City of *London* did on that day declaim against the Corruptions of the Stage, and look'd on the same as the just Cause of that dreadful Judgment: and therefore when I penned this Discourse I was the better satisfied to find so many of the most eminent Men in the Nation concurring in the same Opinion. Neither hath this been published from the Pulpit only, but also from the Press, as appears in a Book intituled, *A Disswasive from the Play-house, in a Letter occasioned by the Calamity of the Tempest*; and the Words of the same Author. *We have lately felt a sad Instance of God's* Page 14. *Judgments in the terrible Tempest: Terrible beyond any thing of that Kind in Memory or Record. For not to enlarge on the lamentable Wrecks and Ruins, were we not almost swept into a Chaos? Did not Nature*

ture

ture seem to be in her last Agony and the World ready to expire? And if we go on still in such Sins of Defiance, may we not be afraid of the Punishment *of* Sodom, *and that* God *should destroy us with Fire and Brimstone?*

What Impreßion this late Calamity *hath made upon the* Play-house *we may guess by their Acting* Mackbeth *with all its Thun-*

Mackbeth
Page 20.

der and Tempest the same day, where at the mention of the Chimneys being blown down, the Auditors were pleased to clap at an unusual Length of Pleasure and Approbation? And is not the Meaning of this too intelligible? Doth it not look as if they had a mind to out-brave the Judgment &c.? And therefore they who are of a different Opinion should first answer that Author in Print, that the World may see the Force of their Arguments; otherwise they may be ashamed to lurk like Snakes in the Grass, and carp at that in private, which they cannot confute in Publick.

I

I did not indeed imagine that the Stage, after such signal Warning both from God and Man, would ever have presumed to have acted for *Comedy* that which was thus turned into *Tragedy* by Divine Justice; and I was the more concerned to find it observed in *A Representation of the Impiety and Immorality of the English Stage*, (Page 5.) that the Players did within a few days after we felt the late dreadful Storm entertain their Auditors with another ridiculous Representation of what had filled us with so great Horrour, in their Plays called *Mackbeth*, and the *Tempest*, as if they designed in the midst of Judgments to persevere in Mocking the Almighty Power of God, *who alone commands the Winds and the Seas, and they obey him* : and therefore I thought that the least which I could do upon that Occasion, was to make some Reflections on such an audacious Practice.

B   I

The Preface

I cannot but confess that I little expected such Reflections on this Subject, when I made no other observations than what the very Heathens made by the Light of Nature on such Occasions. We make our selves familiar with Thunder, Lightning and Tempest, and yet (a) Caligula the Roman Emperor, who was addicted to many Enormities did hide his Head at the Apprehension hereof. We think we may imitate such Things and go unpunished, while the very Heathens tell us of (b) Salmoneus, that when he made a Bridge of Brass, rode thereon in a Chariot, and threw from thence lighted Torches, in Imitation of Thunder and Lightning; then Jupiter for his Insolence struck him with a Thunderbolt and sent him to Hell. And if we retain different Apprehensions hereof, it is a Sign that some

(a) C. Suetonius, in the Life of Caligula, Sect. 51.

(b) Servius in the 6th Æneid of Virgil; or see any common Dictionary.

ſome profeſſing Chriſtianity are ſunk into a more degenerate Eſtate, than that of Paganiſm.

But the Argument which ſome Men urge to make themſelves ſtupid under Judgments is very inſignificant, becauſe *there were ſeveral Seamen drown'd in the Storm who never were within the Walls of a Play-houſe.* But what then ? The Seamen are the Bulwarks of the Nation, and let them be ever ſo innocent, I think we may look upon their Deaths as a National Judgment. They alſo ſay that *the Twenty two Men who were drown'd in the Boat did no way contribute to the Play-houſe.* It was far from my Thoughts to accuſe them as guilty : But I think their Deaths may make us take Warning. (*a*) When the Angel of God ⟨(*a*) 2 *Sam.* 24. 16, 17.⟩ ſtretched forth his Hand upon *Jeruſalem,* to deſtroy it, it was *David*'s Plea to God, *theſe Sheep what have they done?* and yet he look'd upon it as a Judgment for a Sin which they were not guilty of. But

it

The Preface

(a) 2 Sam. 24.
11.

(b) 1 Cor. 10.
11.

(c) Luk. 13.
1, &c.

it may be said, *that David had* (a) *Warning by God.* And we also have Warning by S. *Paul,* (b) that such *things are Examples, and written for our Admonition.* (c) The *Galilæans* whose Blood *Pilate* mingled with their Sacrifices, and the Eighteen upon whom the Tower in *Siloam* fell, and slew them, were not greater Sinners than other Persons ; but their Deaths were a Warning to the Jews, that *except they did repent they should all likewise perish.*

But *some who were contented that I should mention such things as* Judgments *for* Sin *in general, are angry with me because I was too particular.* The Reason is because I spoke against their beloved and their darling Sin, which they are resolved not to part with. And as this is the Reason, I think they shew but little Sign of Repentance, and *Herod's* Case is the same with theirs, who would not part with his *Herodias* though he was

plainly

The Preface.

plainly reproved for it. If such Men profit not by such particular Discourses, I cannot expect much good from the general Notions of Repentance. These are the Persons whom the Prophet (a) Isaiah describes, *which say to the Seers, see not, and to the Prophets, prophesie not unto us; speak unto us smooth things, prophesie Deceits.* However, as I find by their Uneasiness that this Sermon hath wrought their Conviction, I cannot but hope that it will prove in the End to be the Means of their Conversion.

(a) Isai. 30. 10.

Secondly, Some have been offended because *I did accidentally reflect upon the Comedy called* The Spanish Fryar, (written by Mr. *Dryden) which was only innocently (as they say) designed to expose the Errours of the Romish Priests.* Indeed I grant that the Corruptions of that Clergy cannot be too much exposed, though I think the Methods used upon the Stage not so proper, since they

Sect. 7.

fre-

frequently use such Expressions and A-
ctions, (and even in this (*a*) Play) as will
equally reflect upon all
Perswasions; and the *E-
pilogue* seems worded in general Terms
for the very Purpose. When we confute the *Romish Religion* we should do it
so as not to encourage Profaneness or
Immorality in our own; since this is
rather betraying our Cause, and giving
them a greater Advantage whenever
they are pleased to make their Reflections. Can we think Protestants
oblig'd to vindicate all the Expressions in
that *Comedy*, when one of the
(*b*) Actors begins with a
Curse, and another swears
in the fourth Page? Can any
modest Person be pleased with
his (*c*) Description of Adultery? Or
one who hath any Sense of Religion read
without Blushing the (*d*) Account of a
Woman's Creation, or (*e*) the Character of *Lucifer*? The Story which the
Princess,

(*a*) Pag. 2 and 3.

(*b*) Pag. 1.
lin. 9.
(*c*) Pag. 32.
(*d*) Pag. 47.
(*e*) Pag. 53.

Princess *Leonora* (*f*) gives of   (*f*) P. 49,
her being in love, is both te- and 50.
dious and fulsom, and no way becoming
the Gravity of such a Person. And
therefore we who are Protestants have
no Reason to vindicate such a Play as
this, though written against the Papists.

But in this Case there is another Design at Bottom, namely to destroy all Religion while they only seem to level at
one. And accordingly (as this *Author*,
n his *Don Sebastian*, strikes at the *Bishops*
thro' the Sides of the *Mufti*, and exposeth the *Christian* whilst he speaks of
the *Turk* ; so in the *Spanish Fryar*) he only borrows the name of the *Papist* to
make the *Protestant* appear ridiculous.
And lest we should not rightly appre-
hend his Design, he hath in his Poem,
intituled *Absalom and Achitophel*, obliged
us with a Key to unfold the Meaning of
such Expressions.

For Priests of all Religions are the same.

                  The

The Preface

The Poets know too well that the Transition from one Religion to another is natural, the Application easy, and the Auditors very apt to make an ill Use of general Expressions; and therefore we have too much Reason to suppose that the Reflections which they cast upon others are chiefly intended against our selves.

Thirdly, Some are offended because *I seemed to reflect in my Sermon upon the City of BATH.* As Sect. 9. I have made no Alteration from what I then preach'd, so the Reader may guess whether the Reflections are just or not. I think it not fair to strain the Words beyond the Sence which they will naturally bear, and was surprized to hear that any one should say I did then affirm that the *Bath* Waters had lost their Virtue; when I only said that *God had given great Successes to other Wells and Waters, and also to cold Baths, to their apparent Prejudice:* and we of this City should

ſhould be ingrateful to his Providence if we did not own it to be true. However (I think) we have Cauſe to re-flect on the Inhabitants of *Bath,* ſince they were the firſt Promoters of theſe Plays in the Weſt of *England* ; and had it not been for them we might never have been uneaſy at the Apprehenſions thereof. But ſince ſuch falſe Accounts have been raiſed, and induſtriouſly ſpread abroad, I can only obſerve that the *Father of Lies* ſeems to ſupport the Intereſt of the Play-houſes, and is the Cauſe that ſuch Methods are uſed in their Vindication.

Fourthly, Others are offended that *I ſhould mention ſeveral Vices, as* Swearing, *Curſing,* Blaſphemy, Murders, Adulteries, Idleneſs, *and* Contempt *of* Religion, *to be the Effects of the Stage.* I *gave alſo the Reaſons for ſuch Aſſer-tions at the ſame time.* But they ſay ſuch things were in thoſe Places where neither Comedies nor Tragedies are acted. I never Sect. 12, 13, 14, 15, 16.

C

affirmed

affirmed that this was the fole Cause of thefe Vices, but only one of the Caufes, and occafioned the Increafe of them; and I fhould be very glad if we did not find the Truth of what I then faid from woful Experience. However they who urge this to vindicate the *Play-houfe*, may confider, that tho' the Children of *Ifrael* had formerly committed Idolatry, yet it was no Excufe for the *Golden Calves* which were afterward erected, *the one in Bethel, and the other in Dan.*

Laftly, Others have been offended be-

Sect. 14. caufe *I fpoke againft Mufick, and affirmed that it will affect the Paffions.* They who deny that Mufick will affect what Paffion the Compofer pleafeth, muft be great Strangers to that Science, and fuch who (as I fuppofe) never heard a *Sonata* performed in their Lives. But they who apprehended I fpoke againft Mufick in general, were under a great Mifapprehenfion. I only fpoke againft the Corrup-

tions

tions thereof in the *Play-house*, and not against the Science it self. *The best things corrupted are usually the Worst.* I own *Divine Musick* to be a *Noble Exercise*, which will strangely raise the Affections, and fix the Mind upon Heavenly things, and am well satisfied that the Singing of *Psalms*, *Hymns*, and *Anthems* with a full Consort of Voices is one of the best and most solid Pleasures which this World affords. But though Musick is a noble Science, and (in it self) an harmless Recreation, yet it may be abused: Nay as its Design is to affect the Passions, which may by such Allurements be drawn either to Good or Evil; so it is very liable to be corrupted. And as he is justly reckoned the best *Composer* who can most aptly accomodate his Notes to the Humour of the Words; so when the Words are obscene, or immodest, the Musick raiseth the Passion and makes them leave the greater Impression: This is the Manner

how

how Mufick is corrupted in the *Play-house*, and this is the *Corruption* which I then did fpeak againft. I faid nothing on this *Subject* but what I can prove from feveral Inftances too foul to be tran-fcribed, and perhaps too fcandalous to be concealed; and as I have been almoft furfeited in *viewing their Score*, fo (I think) no one fhould be fond of hear-ing their Performance.

Some were offended becaufe I ufed the Word *Chromatick* in my Sermon. I thought none but Fools would have ri-diculed what they did not underftand, and I did not expect to find fuch among thofe who pretend to fo much Wit I did not fay this was the only Way whereby fuch a Paffion was moved, (I wifh it was) but only mentioned fuch a Method, as moft obvious to the Eye, as well as to the Ear of an *Artift*, being fully explained by Mr. *Simpfon* in his *Compendium of Mufick, pag.* 77, and men-tioned by him as proper for fuch an

Ufe,

Ufe, *pag.* 114. And, as for Proof of what I then affirmed, I fhall only look back into the Monthly Colle-ction of Mufick in *October* laft (they who think it worth their while may fearch farther) where there is a Song faid to be Sung at the *Theatre*, begin-ning with thefe Words, *Phillis who knows, &c.* the laft Strain whereof is exactly according to my Defcription, and the four laft Verfes encourages Whoredom, by defcribing a Miftrefs, as one who is Contented, Pleafant, and Beloved. I would tranfcribe the Words, only I am afhamed to blot my Paper. Now if inftead hereof had Mr. *Wilford* the Compofer fent back the Verfes to be corrected by the Poet, he had not expofed himfelf and his Skill: Or had the Poet told us that *Whoredom* was the Way to bring Horrour of Confcience in this World, and the Judgments of God in the other, he had then fpoken Truth, though he might think it would

not

not be accepted at the Play-house, and therefore left it out.

Since all which I can offer must be liable to Misconstructions, I shall only transcribe a Passage out of Mr. *Collier's View of the Stage*, not only to shew that I am not alone in this Opinion, but also in hopes that the Words of another may make some Impression on those whom I am not able to convince.

Conclusion, Page 277. *To go as far in their Excuse as we can, it is probable their Musick may not be altogether so exceptionable as that of the Antients. I do not say this Part of the Entertainment is directly vicious because I am not willing to censure at Uncertainties. Those who frequent the Play-house are the most competent Judges. But this I must say, the Performances of this kind are much too fine for the Place. It were to be wished, that either the Plays were better or the Musick worse. I am sorry to see Art so meanly prostituted. Atheism ought to have nothing charming in its Retinue. It is great*

Pity

to the Reader.

Pity Debauchery should have the Assistance of a fine Hand to whet the Appetite, and play it down.

Now granting the Play-house Musick not vicious in the Composition, yet the Design of it is to refresh the Idea's of the Action, to keep Time with the Poem, and be True to the Subject. For this Reason, among others, the Tunes are generally Airy and Galliardizing. They are contrived on purpose to excite a sportive Humour, and spread a Gayety upon the Spirits; to banish all Gravity and Scruple, and lay Thinking and Reflection asleep. This Sort of Musick warms the Passion, and unlocks the Fancy, and makes it open to Pleasure, like a Flower to the Sun. It helps a luscious Sentence to slide, drowns the Discords of Atheism, and keeps off the Aversions of Conscience. It throws a Man off his Guard, makes way for an ill Impression, and is most commodiously planted to do Mischief. A lewd Play with good Musick is like a Loadstone armed, it draws much stronger than before.

There

The Preface

There is one thing I cannot but obferve, tho' it is very ridiculous: I have been tax'd by fome Perfons of great Sence and Ingenuity (in their own Conceit) for *fpeaking Blafphemy* in my Sermon. This is an heavy Charge, and juftly deferves an heavy Punifhment.

Sect. 12. But thus they prove it: I affirmed, that *Blafphemies were often the Effect of the Stage.* Now becaufe I mentioned the *Word Blafphemy*, therefore they would perfwade the World I *fpoke Blafphemy.* If this is the tender Regard they have for my Reputation, it is eafy to guefs what I muft expect from fuch *Wits,* if the Printing hereof fhould provoke their Patience, and turn their Kindnefs into Cruelty. If this is a good Proof for their Affertion, the Clergy who happen to read Prayers on the 14th of *May* in the Afternoon, when it is not *Sunday,* are liable to *Athaliah's* Fate in the *firft Leffon,* and may like her be put to Death for fpeaking *Treafon*; and I am

per-

to the Reader.

perſwaded that no one thinks he hazards his Neck when he doth only diſcharge his Duty. But if this is no Proof, they might be aſham'd (were they not Friends to the Play-houſe) who take ſuch a Liberty of Speech; and as they imitate the Devil in *Lying*, ſo do they alſo in theſe *Accuſations*, leſt any thing ſhould be wanting to compleat their Character.

I am ſenſible that I have treſpaſſed upon the Readers Patience, by ſo long a Preface, and therefore I muſt, and do crave his Pardon for the ſame, and only take this Opportunity to deſire ſuch as are ſoberly inclined, to pray to God, that the Publiſhing this Sermon may anſwer the End which I aimed at in the Preaching thereof; and if they find their Petitions granted, let them give God the Glory, and own themſelves obliged to thoſe Men whoſe Cenſures and Aſperſions cauſed it to be Printed.

ARTHUR BEDFORD.

D

Serious Reflections

ON THE

STAGE.

IN A

SERMON, &c.

2 Tim. Chap. II. Ver. 16. *But shun pro-*
fane and vain bablings; for they will in-
crease unto more Ungodliness.

THERE are many Vices in
Conversation which this Text
adviseth us to avoid, but I
shall at present only apply the same, in
reference to the *publick Actings* of the
Stage, in *Comedies* and *Tragedies*, and o-
ther Diversions of the same Nature,
and endeavour to shew, that we ought

D 2   to

to shun *these profane and vain Bablings,*
since, if we frequent them, *they will increase unto more Ungodliness.*

2. In order to this it may be thought
requisite that I should prove these things
to be *profane amd vain Bablings.* But
since this is as evident as that the Sun
shines at *Noon-day,* since no-one in this
Age, except Persons of lewd Morals
and a reprobate Sense, denies it; I think
the Matter too notorious to be at this
time insisted on, and only desire such who
doubt the Truth hereof, that they would
seriously peruse *The View of the Immorality
and Profaneness of the* English *Stage, together with the Sense of Antiquity upon this
Argument, by* Mr. Jeremiah Collier; and
also a smaller Treatise, intituled, *A Representation of the Impiety and Immmorality
of the* English *Stage, with Reasons for putting a Stop thereto, and some Questions address to those who frequent the Play-houses;*
in both which Books, and especially in
the former, it is fully proved, That the
Mis-

Misbehaviour of the *Stage*, in respect to Morality and Religion, is *Intolerable*, and doth far exceed the Examples of the former, and even of the Heathen Ages and Poets ; and the Liberties which they take are even offensive to the Profession of Christianity: which plainly appears from their *lewd and filthy Communication* ; their *Swearing, Cursing, Blasphemy, Profaneness*, and *lewd Application of Scripture* ; their *Abuse of the Clergy*, in order to make the Religion (which they profess) become vile and contemptible ; and also their *giving great Characters to Libertines*, or Persons who scruple no Vice or Immorality, and bringing them off with Honour and Success. These things are too gross to be named in a Pulpit, and too scandalous to be concealed from the World. These things are not only proved from what they have acted on the *Stage*, where they may be supposed to use the greater Freedom, (because Words spoken may not always be remembred, and

and cannot so well be prov'd) ; but especially from the *Plays* which they have the Impudence to print, where the Sentences stand upon Record, to their perpetual Shame , and where, in common Prudence, it might be thought they would be more cautious. In short, Their Actings are chiefly designed to gratify such Persons as are of vicious and debauched Principles, *who fear not God, and regard not Man* , since from such it is that they have their Wealth. Hence it is that their Poets seldom scruple to speak *Blasphemy*, rather than lose a *Fancy*, and to affront their *God*, whilst they adore their *Mistress* : And hence it is that they look upon the Regulating of the *Play-houses*, in order to keep them within the Bounds of Modesty, and Religion to be the greatest Prosecution, and which may in the end prove the Suppressing of them. For as they have given a just Scandal to all good Men ; so, if they had not such Acts and Ex-

pressions

preſſions which will pleaſe the bad, they muſt fall at once, and Neceſſity will compel them to take other Employments. I ſhall not therefore ſpend any time in proving theſe things to be *profane and vain Bablings*, but endeavour to ſhew you the Reaſons which ſhould induce us to avoid them, and eſpecially that which is mentioned in the *Text*; becauſe if they are encouraged *they will increaſe unto more Ungodlineſs.*

3. And here I cannot but own that it is a great Satisfaction for me to obſerve, That this hath been alſo the Opinion of the *Grand-Jury*, the *Repreſentatives* of our City at the *General Quarter-Seſſions* of the Peace, who in their Preſentment to the *Mayor* and *Aldermen*, the ſixth Day of *December* laſt, did very pathetically expreſs the great Apprehenſions which they had of theſe Evils breaking in upon us in a worſe Manner than formerly, which (if permitted) *would occaſion an increaſe of Impiety, exceedingly eclipſe the good Order and*

and Government of this City, corrupt and debauch our Youth, and utterly ruin many Apprentices and Servants, already so unruly and licentious, that they are with great Difficulty kept under any reasonable Order and Government by their Masters. And as they have expressed their Desire, that an effectual Care should be taken to remedy those Evils, so they have likewise freed themselves from the publick Guilt, which by their Silence or Negligence would have lain upon them. They have *kept themselves pure*, so as *not to be Partakers with other Mens Sins*, and done their Endeavour to divert the *Judgments of God*, which he might otherwise have inflicted on a City or a Kingdom, for the Wickedness of those who dwell therein. And as they have discharged their Duty in this Matter, so I cannot but hope that the Inhabitants of this City will have some Regard to this Presentment, and practise also the Advice of the Apostle, which is to *shun* these *profane and vain Bablings*;

Bablings ; for they will increase unto more Ungodliness.

4. To this End, let us first consider the *Precepts* and *Examples of the Primitive Christians.*

Collier's View of the Stage , from pag. 250. to 276.

It is very remarkable that all the *Antient Fathers* have spoken very much against the *Plays* , which were used both in *Rome* and in *Greece,* and if we did quote all which hath been said by them upon this Subject, we must transcribe a great part of their Works, since they have written some particular *Books,* as well as *Homilies* or *Sermons* upon this Occasion. (a) *Lactantius* wondered at the Practice of the *Heathen Philosophers*

(a) *Lactantius,* Book 6. chap. 20.

who were present at the Actings of such *Publick Interludes,* and saith that *because they are the publick Allurements of Vices, and do so effectually prevail to the Corrupting of Mens Minds, they ought to be suppress : especially because they are not only unprofitable in bringing us to Hea-*

E *ven,*

ven, but also very pernicious in sending *us*
to *Hell*. And *(b)* in ano-
ther Place he asks this
Question, *Who would not look upon that*
Man to be very wanton and wicked who should
suffer such Acts in his own House? And then
he adds, that *there is no Difference whether*
we are guilty of Lasciviousness alone at Home,
or encourage it by frequenting the same pub-
lickly *in the Theatre.* S. Cy-
prian saith, that *Adultery*
is learnt while these things
are seen, and a Matron who goes chast to
behold such Sights, returns Home with a
*corrupt and debauched Mind. Here (*saith
he*) Wickedness is beheld, and that willingly*
with Delight. What then cannot such
Actions perswade others to do? And therefore he adviseth us to *consider whether a*
Person can be either Innocent or Modest,
who is present at such things.

(b) *Lactantius,*
Book 6. chap. 21.

(c) *Cyprian's*
Epistle to *Donatus.*

(d) Dr. Cave's *Pri-*
mitive Christianity,
Book 2. ch. 2. p. 32.

5. And as the *(d)* Pri-
mitive *Christians* did constantly urge the Necessity
of

of abstaining from these Places, so such as owned themselves to be Christians did as conscientiously follow their Advice. They went not to the *Publick Feasts*, nor frequented the *Shews* which were made for the Diversion and Entertainment of the People; and this was so publickly known, that the Heathen charged it upon them as Part of their Crime. The Heathen (*e*) in the Beginning of *Minutius Fælix* complains of this, That

(*e*) Pag. 34. *Oxford* Edition.

the Romans *governed and enjoyed the World, while the Christians in the mean time were careful and mopish, abstaining from such Pleasures, they visited not the Shews, nor were present at the* Pomps, *they frequented not the publick Feasts, but abhorred all such kinds of Diversions;* which *Octavius* the Christian grants to be true, when he pleaded their Defence, and saith, in Answer to this Charge, (*f*) that *since they were indued with Modesty and Sobriety, they had just Cause to abstain*

(*f*) pag. 106

E 2

ſtain from thoſe evil *Pleaſures*, their *Pomps and Shews*, and to condemn them as hurtful *Allurements*. And he gives this Reaſon, that *in thoſe Acts and Scenical Repreſentations their filthy Communication is as great as their Madneſs, while the Actors ſpeaking of Adulteries incite them, and the Stage-Players by deſcribing of Luſt, do inflame their Hearers.* In ſhort, they thought they could not be preſent at theſe Plays without great Sin and Shame, without affronting their Modeſty, and offering a Diſtaſte and Horrour to their Minds. They look'd upon the publick Sports and Paſtimes of thoſe Days, as the Scenes not only of Folly and Lewdneſs, but of great Impiety and Idolatry, as Places where the *Devil* eminently ruled, and reckoned all his Votaries who came thither.

Dr. *Cave's* Primitive *Chriſtianity*.

6. And as they thought it a great Crime to be preſent at ſuch *Sports*, ſo they look'd upon it as contrary to their *Baptiſmal Vow*. At the time that Perſons

ſons were baptized, they were among others asked theſe two (*g*) Queſtions : *Doſt thou renounce the Devil, and all his Works, Powers and Services?* And *Doſt thou renounce the World, and all its Pomps and Pleaſures?* And to each of theſe Queſtions the Party anſwered, ſaying, *I do renounce them.* And each of theſe Queſtions they ſuppoſed to be directly levelled againſt the Theatres. St. *Cyril*, (*h*) expounding the Word *Pomps*, expreſsly tells us, that thereby is meant, *the Sights and Sports of the Publick Stage.* (*i*) Thoſe *Pompous Spectacles , Plays ,* and *Scenical Repreſentations* exhibited in the *Roman Theatres*, which becauſe they were ſo Lewd, Cruel, and Impious, it was an early Cuſtom for the *Primitive Biſhops,* and *Fathers* of the *Church*, in their Diſcourſes to the *Baptized Perſons*, ſtrictly to

(*g*) Apoſtolical Conſtitutions, Book 7. chap. 42. pag. 993.

(*h*) St. *Cyril* of *Jeruſalem* , Catech. Myſt. 1. Pag. 510.
(*i*) Dr. *Bray* upon the Church Catechiſm, Lect. 19.

to enjoyn them, not to frequent, or so much as to be once present, or seen at such Places. They reckoned (*k*) all those *Pomps* as *Allurements* to *Vice*, and those Houses as so many *Synagogues* of *Satan*, and consequently by *renouncing the World and the Devil*, they also renounced the same. Accordingly (*l*) *Tertullian* tells us of a *Christian Woman who going to the Theatre was there possessed by the Devil, and when the evil Spirit, at his casting out, was asked how*

(*k*) It may be observed from S. *Cyril*, that the Word *Pompa* is used to signify the *Acts* of the *Stage*; though that is not its only Meaning. It may also be observed that the Word was used both by Heathens and by Christians. The *Heathen*, in *Minutius Felix*, charged the *Christians* with this pretended Crime *Non Pompis interestis*; and the *Christian* confessed, the Charge, saying, *Merito malis Voluptatibus, et Pompis vestris, et Spectaculis abstinemus*. And therefore as the Word *Pomps* is expresly used in our Renunciation of Baptism, and in our Church-Catechism; as we ratify and vow the same in our own Persons at Confirmation; and as the Word is of a *Greek* Original, so I think there is reason to take it according to the Interpretation of a *Greek* Father, and not confine it only to the Sence in which the *Latins* often use it,

(*l*) *Lib. de Spectaculis*, Pag. 701. *Edit.* Basil. 1562.

how he durst set upon a Christian? he presently answered, *I did but what was fit and just, for I found her upon my own Ground.* Neither is this the only Instance which he there mentions, but he saith, that *there are other Examples of those who while they held Communion with the Devil, by frequenting these Shews, did at the same time fall away from the Faith.* And then he adds, *For no Man can serve two Masters, what Communion hath Light with Darkness? and what Fellowship hath Life with Death? We ought* (saith he) *to hate those Meetings and Assemblies of the Heathen, because there the Name of God is blasphemed.* And then he adds, *Do you doubt in that Minute in which you shall be present at the Synagogue of Satan, that all the Angels do look down from Heaven and behold every one who speaks the Blasphemy, and who hears it, who lends a Tongue, and who lends an Ear to the Devil to be employed against God? Will you not therefore avoid that Seat of the Enemies of Christ, that infectious Chair, and*
that

that *Air* which is polluted with wicked and profane *Discourse?* And therefore since our *Modern Plays,* which are acted in the Play-houses, are no less inferiour to the *Antient* ones in *Impiety* and *Lewdness* than they are in *Shew* and *Pomp,* we may suppose those *Antient Fathers,* if they had lived in our Days, would have expressed their Resentments now, in the same Language which they did then. Since they have such a malignant Influence upon Faith and Manners (as is owned almost by all Persons, and is generally complained that they have) they may be reckoned among the Works of the *Devil,* as well as those of former *Ages,* and ought not be encouraged by such as call themselves *Christians.* And since we also have been *baptized,* and have promised to *renounce the Devil and all his Works,* as well as the *vain Pomps and Vanities of this wicked World,* and all *the sinful Lusts of the Flesh, so that we will not follow nor be led by them:* We

ought

ought as they to confider the Nature of our *Baptifmal Vow*, and (m) be- (m) Prov. 2. ware left we break that *Co-* 17. *venant* which we folemnly made *with our God.*

7. Secondly, Let us confider, that *God feems to enter into Judgment with us for thefe things.* There are fome particular Punifhments which carry in them the Nature of the Offence, infomuch that a Man may not only fee that it is the immediate *Finger of God*, but alfo what it is which forceth him to ftrike ; and if we will not take notice of fuch things, we have Caufe to fear what the *Pfalmift* faith, Pfal. 28. 5. *Becaufe they regard not the Works of the Lord, nor the Operations of his Hands, he fhall deftroy them, and not build them up.* Whilft fome among us have been acting of *Tragedies upon the Stage,* and others have been diverted with the *Mock-fhews* of *Battles, Blood,* and *Murder,* in the mean time God hath permitted *the Sword to be*

F *drawn*

drawn in other Nations, of which we (tho' at a Distance) do feel the Smart; and therefore it is pity that such who are delighted with these *Scenes* did not go into the *Army,* in order to be Spectators of the same: and if the Sword is not drawn in the Heart of the Nation, and we are not involved in a Civil War, no Thanks are due to such who make a Jest of these things; but rather to the Mercy of God, and the Supplications of such who stand in the *Gap,* to *turn away his wrathful Indignation that we perish not.* Whilst some among us have set up *Mock-Princes* upon the *Stage,* God hath permitted our neighbouring Enemy to set up Pretenders to the Crowns of *England, Spain,* and *Poland,* thereby involving us in a Bloody War, and endeavouring as much as possible to increase our Divisions among our selves, that so this poor Kingdom may not stand, but be brought to Desolation. Whilst some among us have been acting the Part of a *Spanish Fryar,*

Fryar, they have been acting their Parts, to the utmost of their Power, against the *Protestant Interest*, and perhaps are the only Persons who have prevented a Revolution in that Nation, which was the only visible Means of settling us again in Peace and Safety. And if we go on in this Manner, we have reason to fear that God will go on to punish us according to our Iniquities; and tho' he hath given us this last Summer some remarkable Successes, yet he is able whenever he pleaseth to turn the Scale; and it ought to be in our Minds, that *he who saved the Children of* Israel *out of the Hand of the* Egyptians, *afterwards destroyed those that repented not.*

8. But that which (I think) ought most sensibly to affect us of this City is this: That these are the Persons who in their Plays called the *Tempest*, and *Mackbeth*, have not only represented themselves in the Shape of *Devils*, the dreadful Executioners of *God's* Vengeance

in

in the other World, but also presumed
to imitate his *Judgments* in this, such as
Thunder, Lightning, Rain, Wind, Storms,
and *Shipwrecks*: and therefore we ought
(unless we are wholly stupid) to ob-
serve, that when in the Year 1703, they
came to the Neighbourhood of this
City, and some of our Inhabitants encouraged their Proceedings, by being
present at their Acts, *God* was pleased
to shew us, the 26th of *November* following, that *he would not be mock'd*, by
visiting us with such a Storm of Wind,
and Inundation of the Sea, which was
a Judgment sufficient to make us know
what we might for the future expect, if
we should again encourage such People
among us, who do thus provoke him to
Anger.   Since this, such Persons as these
have again acted within this City, and
design (as we have Cause to fear) to
settle among us.   Accordingly God was
pleased, on *Saturday* the 21st of *October*
last, to visit us again with another violent
Storm,

Storm, wherein some Vessels were sunk, and others in the utmost Danger. Since that, he was pleased to visit us with another, at which time Twenty two Men were lost in one Boat; and since that, with another, which was severely felt by our *West-India* Fleet, and what Damage they have sustained, or how many men are lost thereby, must be left to Time alone to discover. Neither are these the only Tokens of this Nature which God hath sent among us. And therefore should these Men be encouraged to carry on their pernicious Designs, by our being present at their Acts: We must be look'd on as a stupid and senseless People, who will take no Warning until *Vengeance come upon us to the uttermost.* And as we depend more particularly upon the Providence of God in regulating the Winds and Seas, so we have greater Reason to tremble at the Effects of his Wrath when we thus provoke him.

9. Neither

9. Neither are the Effects of God's Displeasure visible in this alone, but also in a *Neighbouring City*; who having in the Year 1703. built up such a *Synagogue for Satan*, supposing that it might increase their Trade, did not only feel with us the Effects of God's Anger in that first dreadful Storm, but they have since complained that they have no Command of their Children, Apprentices and Servants as they formerly had : and, as to their Secular Interest, have found it not according to their Expectation. Our *Gracious Queen* (whom *God* long preserve) was with them, with the Court, before the said Nusance was erected, but they have not been there ever since, tho' greatly expected this last Summer : and *God* hath given great Successes to other Wells and Waters, and also to cold Baths, to their apparent Prejudice ; and this thing which they thought would have been for their Wealth, seems to make *God* become their Enemy, and may con=

conſequently prove to them an Occaſion of falling. And therefore ſince we **may** juſtly look upon theſe things as viſible **Marks** of God's Diſpleaſure, ſo the **Misfortune** of others as well as our own ſhould teach us to·beware, left we alſo feel the Effeᶜts thereof.

10. Thirdly, Let us conſider the Reaſon which the Apoſtle urgeth in the **Text.** If we ſhould encourage this Evil it will make Way for more ; and *If we do not ſhun theſe profane and vain Bablings, they will increaſe unto more Ungodlineſſ.* In vain may we pretend to a *Reformation of Manners,* and a *Regulation of our Youth,* when ſuch Temptations lie in their Way, which, if frequented, will certainly debauch them. In vain is the *Bee-Hive* the *Seal* of our *Corporation* for the Poor, as a Sign of their Induſtry, whilſt other Places in this City ſhall be frequented, which encourage them to Idleneſſ. In this Caſe we expeᶜt that Youth will follow that which is moſt

agree-

agreeable to their corrupt Inclinations; and whilst the Temptations are equally strong on either Side, and the Heart of Man is fully set in him to do Evil, we cannot but expect that the Consequences hereof will be fatal to some, and the *Devil* will not be wanting to make use of such Opportunities to tempt Men to sin, until they are involved in eternal Destruction. The sad Experience hereof made *Menander* an Heathen Poet say, that *Evil Communications do corrupt good Manners*, which was so certain and true, that it became a Proverb in *Greece*, and afterwards assented unto by S. *Paul* who inserts the same into the *Holy Scripture* with a particular Caution of his own left we should be deceived by such Insinuations. And therefore it may not be amiss to suppose that S. *Paul*, directing his Epistle to *Ephesus*, which was a City bordering upon *Greece*, where the Comedies of *Aristophanes* were frequently acted, which (though some of them

are

are Profane and Atheiſtical, yet) come not up to the Impiety of our preſent Stage, might have a particular Reference to theſe Enormities, when he adviſed *Timothy* to *ſhun profane and vain Bablings*, *becauſe they would increaſe unto more Ungodlineſs*; and if this was the Cauſe of Ungodlineſs increaſing in an Heathen Country (*n*) whoſe Manners were *looſe* and *profligate*, *wanton* and *effeminate*,

(*n*) *Strabo* Geogr. Book 14. pag. 41.

and who made an Injunction, ſaying, *Let none of ours be thrifty*, ſo that they could hardly be worſe; what muſt we expect in a City *profeſſing Chriſtianity*, and *making at leaſt a Shew of Religion?*

11. But it is not ſufficient to ſpeak of the Increaſe of Ungodlineſs in general; and therefore I ſhall mention ſome particular Vices which ſeem in great Meaſure to be the Effects of our preſent Stage and their Acts.

12. The firſt is the *Profaning of God's Name by Swearing, Curſing, and Blaſphemy.*

G Of

Of these there are innumerable, and intolerable Examples in our modern Plays, as they have been fully expofed by other Authors; which are fpoken as Patterns for the *Bullies* of the Age to imitate. Neither are they contented with fuch as are more common, becaufe it looks as if they had not Wit enough to affront God more effectually than their Neighbours, but are daily inventing new Fafhions of this Nature, as if the Play-houfe was only a Forge to hammer out new Pieces of Armour whereby to rebel againft God, and bid him defiance. And therefore it is obfervable that when our *Englifh* Stage took a greater Liberty than had been known in former Ages, it foon infected the Officers of the Army, who went to hear them; and they (like Perfons fick of the *Plague*) as often as they marched, carried the Diftemper from City to City, which firft began in their Regiments, and fo overfpread the Nation. And there is another

ther

ther thing remarkable, that (in order, as they think, to avoid the Law) they change the Letter, and keep to the Meaning (as by putting the Word *Gad* inftead of *God*) and therefore are in this Refpect as guilty of the Sin as fuch who never mince the Matter, fince it is not the *Words*, but the *Senfe*, which makes an *Oath* or *Curfe*. And what they do in this manner, can ferve for no other Purpofe than to teach their Hearers fuch Methods, whereby they may be guilty of the Sin, and flatter themfelves that they fhall efcape a temporal Punifhment.

13. Secondly, *Murthers* are often the Effects of the Stage. Many of our modern *Tragedies* are defigned to fhew the Succefs of fuch who think their Wills to be a Law ; who Hector at, Quarrel with, Fight and Deftroy all before them. To thefe it is that the Actors pay Refpect, give them great Titles, admire their Courage, and praife their

Vices,

Vices, inftead of Virtues. Such Sights, Bloodfhed, and Murther, being fhewn on a Stage, do by Degrees occafion the Spectators to be cruel and outragious; and Men (if I may fo fpeak) do there learn to be *Inhuman*. Such Perfons who are in the Heat of Youth, and are of a proud and paffionate Temper, immediately think they may act the fame Parts upon the publick Stage of the World, and come off with the fame Succefs, until they are convinced of their Errour when perhaps it is too late. And it was very obfervable that the greateft *Perfecutions* which were ever raifed againft the *Chriftians* were begun and carried on in *Heathen Rome*, where they had their *Theatres*, and their *Tragedies* were moft frequently acted. This made them more cruel, and delight in Bloodfhed, infomuch that at laft the Martyrdom of the Saints became their Diverfion, and Chriftians were in reality brought forth to be devoured by wild Beafts,

to

to make Paftime for thofe who had pleas'd themfelves with fuch Refemblances. And fince the Reformation, it is as remarkable that the dreadful Perfecutions againft the Proteftants, and all their Defigns to deftroy our Religion, have either been begun, or at leaft carried on and promoted by that City. This is that *great Whore* who hath been diverted by the *Theatres*, *Carnivals*, and *Jubilees*; and as fhe was addicted to fuch Sports and Paftimes, it may be the lefs wondered at, that in all Ages fhe hath made her felf fo *drunk with the Blood of the Saints.*

14. Thirdly, *Adulteries* and *Whoredoms* are the common Effects of the Stage. The notorious Immodefty both in words and Actions which are there heard and feen, the filthy Songs which are there Sung, and the Mufick framed by the Compofers with fuch Notes as will moft affect the Paffions, are but as fo many Temptations to Luft, and ferve

serve only to inftruct the Hearers how to carry on their own filthy Defigns, that fo when they go from thence in a mix'd Company of both Sexes, they may go (if poffible) to a worfe Place, and be the real Actors of what was thus reprefented. This is fo evident that a Perfon who only views *the Score of their Mufick*, without hearing the Performance, may obferve that where there are *foft Chromatick-Notes joyn'd with a flat Key*, in order to ftrike gently upon the Paffions together with their Strings, they are defigned to ufher in fomething that is immodeft, or at leaft to ftir up *Luft*, under the *Name* of *Love*, and do as certainly prepare for fuch Expreffions, as the *Difcords* in their Mufick prepare for a *Clofe*; which looks as if *Mufician*, *Poet*, and *Actor* did ufe the beft of their Skill only to ridicule the *Seventh Commandment*, and expofe the Authority of that God who gave it.

15. Fourthly, *Idleneß* is the common Effect of the Stage. It is with great Difficulty that Youth are kept to Labour and Induſtry, and therefore all Temptations to the contrary are prejudicial. But when *ſuch* leave their *Callings* to go to the *Plays*, it is but ſeldom that the Maſters have any Command of thoſe who are under them. They have a ſtrange Inclination to go thither again and again, and ſo all neceſſary Buſineſs ſhall be neglected, to gratify their Fancy. Beſides it is uſually late before the Plays are ended, and if the Company is large, the Heat of the Place will make them thirſty. This expoſeth them to go to *Taverns* and *Ale-houſes* with ſome of their Companions, and then it is ſo much the later before they return Home. By this Means Families are diſordered, and forced to keep unſeaſonable Hours, and therefore they cannot be ſo early about their lawful Callings. After this ſuch Youth think themſelves too good to
be

be confined, and weary of the Station in which God hath fet them ; and thus the Principles of Idlenefs and Extravagance are ftrangely infufed into fuch People as refort to thefe *Acts*, which often tends to their utter Ruin.

16. Laftly, *Contempt of all Religion* is too often the Effect of the Stage. As fuch Perfons feldom fcruple to fpeak the moft horrid Blafphemies, as a Diverfion and Entertainment to their Company ; fo we cannot expect that fuch who hear thefe Things can be reckoned Men who have any Senfe of the Honour of God, or Dread of his Judgments. Alas! nothing is more common for fuch than to affront their Maker , and make a *Goddefs* of their *Miftrefs*, to think of no *Heaven* except to be in her *Company*, and no Hell but to be kept from her. This and much more, which one would tremble to relate, is the Language of the Play-houfe, and indeed fome of the beft.

beſt. Mr. *Collier*, treating of this (*o*) Subject, quotes out of the printed Plays ſeveral Examples (*p*) where the Service of
God in a Church, and Prayer is ridiculed,
where they (*q*) ſwear by *Mahomet*, (*r*) contemn even Heaven it ſelf, and (*ſ*) give
the Preference to the *Turkiſh* Paradiſe,
(*t*) where they make a Jeſt of
their *Baptiſmal Vow*, (*u*) where
they look upon Providence to
be a ridiculous Superſtition,
and affirm (*x*) that none but
Blockheads pretend to Religion. In one of their Plays,
(*y*) like *Lucian* and *Celſus*,
they deride the Reſurrection :

(*o*) Chap. 2.
page 56, *&c.*
(*p*) pag.60.
(*q*) pag. 61.
(*r*) pag. 81.
(*ſ*) pag.61.
(*t*) pag. 63.
(*u*) pag. 81.
(*x*) pag.78,
and 147.
(*v*) pag. 66.
(*z*) pag. 68.
(*i*) pag. 67.

One (*z*) ſpeaks againſt the *Immortality
of the Soul*, and another (*a*) brings in
a lewd *Italian Proverb* for Authority, in
Contempt of the *Holy Scriptures*. And
that which makes it the worſe is that
theſe things are covered over with the
Strains of *Wit* and *Fancy*, which like the
Bait, is uſeful only to cover the Hook
H   that

that it may not be perceived until they are deſtroyed who are taken therewith: or like *Poiſon in a Cordial*, which may work inſenſibly, and will delight, and ſo deſtroy the Vitals of Religion, before it is diſcovered.

17. Since therefore theſe *profane and vain Bablings* do (as the Apoſtle ſaith) *increaſe unto more Ungodlineſs*; this ſhould exhort all ſuch who pretend to a Senſe of Religion, or Love to their own Souls, to avoid the ſame.

See *Ameſius, De Conſcientiâ*, Lib. 5. Cap. 10. Quæſt. 7. (*b*) *Euſebius*'s *Eccleſiaſtical Hiſtory*, Lib. 3. Cap. 28. *alias* 25.

Such *evil Communications* will *corrupt good Manners*, and therefore *let us not be deceived*. When (*b*) Saint *John* the Apoſtle ſaw *Cerinthus* the Heretick in the ſame Bath with him, he immediately withdrew himſelf, and adviſed others ſo to do, leſt the Judgments of God ſhould overtake them for being in ſuch Company: and certainly we have as much reaſon to take his Advice, in relation to the

Play-

Play-house. What *Tertullus* falsly said of St. *Paul*, may be true of such *Actors*; Act. 24. 5. *We have found such Men to be Pestilent Fellows,* λοιμόν, *a Plague.* And therefore we should deal by them as we do by such as are afflicted with that Distemper. Now if we are afraid of such a Disease which will only *kill the Body,* how much more should we fear that Contagion, which, if not prevented, will *destroy both Body and Soul in Hell?* Let us remember the Charge which God gives us in the Text, and not only there, but also in other Places of Scripture. Thus it is, *Eph.* 5. 11, 12. *Have no Fellowship with the unfruitful Works of Darkneß, bnt rather reprove them. For it is a Shame even to speak of those things which are done of them in Secret.* So *Prov.* 14. 14, &c. *Enter not into the Path of the Wicked, and go not in the Way of evil Men. Avoid it, paſs not by it, turn from it, and paſs away. For they sleep not except they have done Mischief,*

H 2   *and*

and their Sleep is taken away unless they cause some to fall. For they eat the Bread of Wickedness, and drink the Wine of Violence. And *Psal.* 1. 1, 2. *Blessed is the Man that hath not walked in the Counsel of the Ungodly, nor stood in the Way of Sinners, and hath not sate in the Seat of the Scornful. But his Delight is in the Law of the Lord, and in his Law doth he exercise himself day and Night.* If these Places were not frequented they would fall of course, and when the Hopes of their Gains were gone, they would betake themselves to something more reputable for a Livelihood. However if some *Men* should be so obstinate and refractory, as to take no wholsom Advice in this Matter; yet one would think that such *Women*, who have any Regard to their Reputation, will shun those Places. One would think that such filthy Discourse would be very affronting in Conversation, and not endured by any *Lady* who

values

values her Credit. And one would think it ftrange that fuch Liberties which they would juftly refent in private Converfation, fhould entertain and pleafe them on the Publick Stage. In fhort, their going thither feems no more than fpending their Money to hear themfelves abufed, and their Modefty affronted; and in fuch a Cafe it is much better to ftay at Home. To fuppofe that fuch can like it, is a grofs Reflection upon their Virtue; and therefore I fhould rather hope they will take Care not to expofe themfelves.

18. To conclude. As I have taken this Occafion to fpeak my Thoughts concerning this Evil, I have freed my felf from having any Share of the Guilt, which may be contracted thereby, and the evil Confequences which may attend it: and hope alfo others whom it doth concern, will free themfelves by ufing all poffible Endeavours to prevent that which may occafion fo much *Ungodlinefs.*

godliness. That Text, *Ezek.* 33. 9. is a great Satisfaction to me ; *Nevertheless if thou warn the Wicked of his Way to turn from it : if he do not turn from it, he shall die in his Iniquity, but thou hast delivered thy Soul.* And therefore let the Sin lie at their Door who will take no Warning, and if *God's* Judgments should overtake those who are guilty, their Blood must light upon their own Heads.

19. I shall therefore only request these two Particulars.

First, That such *Books* may be disperst through this City, which give us a true and lively *Representation of the Impiety and Immorality* of the *English Stage.* What is read in Print may perhaps make a deeper Impression than what is delivered from the Pulpit : However both together may be the more effectual.

20. And *Secondly*, That such Persons who after all that can be said will take no Warning, may be particularly

cularly taken-notice of, as Perfons who *fear not God*, and *regard not Man*, who value not *His* Judgments, nor their own Reputation; who fide with fuch as are bold in *Sin*, and openly addicted to the Service of the *Devil*; and who, though they *are made whole* from the Effect of the late Storms, do continue to *fin more* and more. until they provoke God to fend *a worfe thing upon us.* This is the Advice of the Apoftle; 2 *Theff.* 3. 15, 16. *And if any obey not our Word, by this Epiftle, Note that Man, and have no Company with him, that he may be afhamed. Yet count him not as an Enemy, but admonifh him as a Brother.* And let us pray to God to give us his Grace that we may delight our felves in his Commandments, that Singing his Praifes may be our beft Mufick, and Hearing his Word our greateft Diverfion; and we may fay with *David,* Pfal. 119. 113. *I hate vain Thoughts,*

or

or them that imagine evil Things: *but thy Law do I love.* Thefe are Enjoyments which will leave no Sting of Confcience behind, but will revive our Souls in the greateft Affliction; and whilft we taft of them in this World, they will be but as Earnefts of far greater, which we fhall enjoy in the World to come.

F I N I S.

A Copy of the Presentment of the Grand Jury for the City of Bristol, *which was mentioned in the Third Section of the former Sermon.*

To the Right Worshipful Francis Whitchurch, *Esq; Mayor, and the Worshipful the Aldermen, Her Majesty's Justices of the Peace for the City and County of* Bristol, *met at the General Quarter-Sessions of the Peace begun and held the* 3d *of* October, Anno Domini 1704, *and continued by several Adjournments to the* 6th Day *of* December 1704.

I   We

WE the Grand-Jurors for our Sovereign Lady the Queen, for the Body of the County of this City do (as in Confcience and Duty bound) acknowledge the good Endeavours that have been ufed by this Worfhipful Bench, for fome Years paft, to difcourage Immorality and Profanenefs by bringing under Reftraint, and endeavouring to fupprefs thofe evil Methods by which they were promoted and encouraged; fuch as *Mufick-houfes*, and other *Lewd* and *Diforderly Houfes*, the *Exercife* of *Unlawful Games*, the *extravagant Number* of *Ale-houfes*, *Tipling*, or *idle Walking* on the *Lord's Day*, *profane Curfing and Swearing*, *Acting* of *Plays* and *Interludes*; which Endeavours tending to God's Glory, your Zeal and Forwardnefs therein hath juftly gained you the Efteem and Honour of all good People of this City, and the adjacent Counties, to whom you have not only fhewed a good Example, but encouraged

to

to profecute fo good a Work : and we
are alfo with all humble Submiffion
bound to reprefent the fad apprehen-
fions we have of the fame Evils again
breaking in upon us worfe than formerly, by the *Increafe* of the *great Number* of
Tipling-houfes, kept by fuch who in Contempt of Juftice fell Ale without Li-
cenfe, (the *Lord's Day* being much pro-
faned by *Tipling* in *fuch Houfes*) and
alfo by the great Concourfe of People in
publick Places, under pretence of hearing
News on that Day. But that which puts
us more efpecially under thefe *fad Appre-*
henfions, is the late Permiffion given to
the *Publick Stage*, within the Liberties of
this City, from whence fome have conceived hopes it fhall be tolerated always ;
and Countenance (or at leaft Conni-
vance) given to *Acting of Plays and Inter-*
ludes within this City and County, which
(if it fhould be) will exceedingly eclipfe
the good Order and Government of
this City, corrupt and debauch our *Youth*,

and utterly ruin many *Apprentices* and *Servants*, already so *Unruly* and *Licentious*, that they are with great Difficulty kept under any reasonable Order or Government by their Masters.

WE could wish that these our Sad Apprehensions were groundless: But, when in all Ages, *Acting* of *Plays* and *Interludes* hath been attended with all manner of *Profaneness*, *Lewdness*, *Murthers*, *Debauching*, and *Ruining Youth* of *both Sexes*, infusing *Principles* of *Idleness* and *Extravagancy* into all People that resort to them. We hope your Worships seriously will consider of Effectual Methods to prevent them, and with the greatest Zeal and Fervency put the same in Execution, when it is apparent that all the Methods to correct and keep them within modest Bounds (where they are tolerated) have proved ineffectual: And all Wise Men are convinced that there are no Methods of hindering or preventing their Mischiefs, but by totally suppressing

sing them.   Your Worships Task is
not so difficult; Preventing Remedies
being more natural and easy than Pu-
nishing. And we humbly conceive, you
have Reasons more cogent to stir you
up to this Work, than offer themselves
to Cities and Places where they have
been tolerated, abounding with *Gentry*
and *Nobility*, whose *Estates* and *Leisure*
render such Extravagancies more tolerable. But if in such Places their
direful and calamitous Effects have been
so sensibly felt, how much more, in a
City not to be upheld but by Trade and
Industry, will they be insupportable?
We therefore do not doubt but all due
Care will be taken by your Worships
to redress and prevent these *Grievances*,
that a Stop may be put to the further
Progress of *Immorality* and *Profaneness*,
and the Work of *Reformation* carried on,
so earnestly prest by Her Majesty's Proclamation, whose Pious Endeavours
God hath so signally owned in the great
Victories

Victories with which he hath blessed her Arms, and whose glorious Example we doubt not but you will follow, to your lasting Honour and Renown, and the Encouragement and Comfort of all good Citizens.

Walter Chapman.
Daniel Hickman.
Edward Thurston.
Thomas Adderly.
William Galbraith.
Thomas Gadell.
Thomas Yate.
Stephen Peloquin.
Richard Taylor Junior.
James Stewart.
John Scott.
Jeremiah Pearce.

Adver-

Advertisement,

These following *Books*, besides several others, have been lately *Printed* against the *Play-House*,

1. **A** *Short View* of the *Immorality* and *Profaneness* of the *English Stage*, together with the *Sense* of *Antiquity* upon this *Argument*.

2. A *Defence* of the *Short View* of the *Profaneness* and *Immorality* of the *English Stage*.

3. A *Dissuasive* from the *Play-House* in a *Letter* to a *Person* of *Quality*, occasioned by the late *Calamity* of the *Tempest*. These Three by Mr. *Jeremy Collier*.

4. A *Letter* to Mr. *Congreve*, on his pretended *Amendments* of Mr. *Collier's Short View* of the *Immorality* and *Profaneness* of the *English Stage*.

5. A

5. A Representation of the Impiety and Immorality of the *English Stage*, with Reasons for putting a Stop thereto, and some *Questions Address'd* to those who Frequent the *Play-Houses*.

6. *Maxims* and *Reflections* upon *Plays*, Written in *French* by the Bishop of *Meaux*, and now made *English*.

A

SECOND

Advertisement

CONCERNING THE

Profaneness

OF THE

Play-House,

THE *Profaneness* of the *Play-house* near *Bristol* having been lately shewn in an *Advertisement* printed for this purpose, it was believed, and hoped, that the *Players* would have had so much Regard to their *former Promises*, and their *own Reputation*, as to forbear the *Acting* such *Plays*, which have a notorious Tendency to *Immorality* and *Profaneness*, and that they would give no Occasion to the World

B of

of any farther *Advertisement*. But instead of this they so hate to amend, that like *Evil Men, and Seducers* (of whom the Apostle speaks) *they wax worse and worse, deceiving and being deceived*. They are notoriously *rampant* in their *Wickedness* against all Admonitions; and by their late Practice they have fully proved the Charge brought against them in a late Sermon, Pag. 37, that they are *Persons bold in Sin, and openly addicted to the Service of the Devil*; and also that nothing less than a *Total Suppressing* of such *Actings* can work *Reformation*.

Since therefore these things have of late been so fully declared to the World, the Fault lies as much in *those Persons* who *hear them*, as in the *Actors themselves*: and it is evident that none can plead *Ignorance* to excuse their Crime. These are the Men who spend their *Time* and their *Money*, to encourage all manner of *Sin* and *Wickedness*, who openly delight in *Swearing*, *Cursing*, *Blasphemy* and *Profaneness*, who *fear not God, and regard not Man*, and may be look'd upon as Men of *corrupt Minds* and *debauch'd Practices*, who are given over to a *reprobate Sense*, and resolve to go on in *Sin*, until Vengeance comes upon them to the uttermost. These

are

are the Men who rather than fail of encouraging such as ridicule the *Scriptures,* *Virtue and Religion,* do bid *God* defiance, and give *Scandal* to such who are *zealous* for his Honour; and rather than cease from *laughing* at such things for a *Moment,* do run the Danger of being cast into that Place where there shall be *Weeping, Wailing and Gnashing of Teeth* for ever.

For the more full Proof hereof, I shall give the *Reader* a short *Account* of the Play which was acted on *Monday* the 23d of *July* 1705, according to their *Advertisement,* which may cause all sober Persons to blush, not only in behalf of the *Actors* themselves, but also in behalf of such who are delighted to hear them.

Remarks upon the Comedy *called* Love for Love, *as it was acted on* Monday *the* 23d *of* July, *according to their publick* Advertisement.

First, This *Play* hath already been censured by Mr. *Collier* in his *View of the Stage*; and the lame defence of it written afterward by the *Author* did only give an Opportunity for Exposing it farther in Mr. *Collier's Reply.* The *Actors* there-

fore

fore could not but be senfible that this was a *Comedy* publickly known to be *fcandaleus* and *profane*; but nothing of this Nature could prevail upon them to omit it.

Mr. *Collier* particularly tells us of the *Immodefty* hereof, Pag. 4, and Pag. 10, that *Mifs* Prue *is reprefented filly, the better to enlarge her Liberty, and fkreen her Impudence from the publick Cenfure.* He tells us, pag. 24, that *Heathen* Comedians *had no fmutty Songs in their Plays*; but for this the Englifh (*efpecially* Love for Love) *are extreamly fcandalous.* He largely charges this *Comedy*, pag. 74, *&c.* and pag. 83, with *Profanenefs*, in *Abufing of Religion, and the Holy Scriptures*; and, pag. 142, with *reprefenting* Valentine *the* Hero *of the* Play *as a* Perfon *compounded of Vice, a prodigal Debauchee, unnatural and profane, obfcene, fawcy and undutiful*; and *rewarding him at laft, for a Man of Merit, with a Fine Lady, and Thirty Thoufand Pounds:* So that fince this *Comedy* hath been painted in its proper Colours, the Reader may the better excufe it, if I fometimes borrow the Words of the fame Author.

Secondly, The Songs fet to Mufick in this Play are alfo remarkable. The firft which I fhall mention is in pag. 45. The
Words

Words are intolerably *obscene* and *scanda-lous*, with a Mixture of *profane Wit*, to please a Country-man's Fancy; and the Notes are plain and easy, according to his Capacity. The Design hereof is that such Verses may be disperst and sung in Country Places for their Diversion, that the Poison of the Play-house may spread farther than many imagine, and such also may be debauch'd by them, who never came to hear them.

The second Song is in pag. 33. The Design of it is to tell the World that all Women are Whores who were ever tempted: or in their own Language ---

--- *The Nymph may be chast that has never been try'd.*---

This is set for Ladies to learn to sing if they please to complement their own Sex so far; and it is observable that the frequent Repetitions of the Words, as designed by the Composer, do make the Sence the more emphatical.

The Third is in Pag. 61, written in Praise of Whoring and Debauchery. The Musick is indeed too fine for the Words, and the Composer hath shewn his Art, only he wanted to employ it better. The
Tune

Tune is fit for a Lady to learn, and the
Words seem better polished for a nicer
Palate than the rest, for which Reason I
shall venture to transcribe some of them.

Love hates to center in a Point assign'd,
But runs with Joy the Circle of the Mind.
Then never let us chain what should be free.
But for Relief of either Sex agree,
Since Women love to change, and so do we.

Here we have Lewdness in Verse,
though wrapp'd up in cleaner Linnen,
and fine Musick to double the Force of the
Mischief, and drive it stronger upon
Fancy and Practice. And there is no
doubt but many a Fine Woman hath
been insensibly debauch'd when they learn
such Songs for their 𝖇𝖊𝖙𝖙𝖊𝖗 𝕭𝖗𝖊𝖊𝖉𝖎𝖓𝖌, and
which hath proved the Ruin of some
Families. Thus Vice and Profaneness
corrupts a most noble Science, spreads
with Delight, both in City and Country,
among Gentle and Simple; and the Original of all lies at the *Play-house* Door.

Fourthly, The Comedy it self is notoriously scandalous, *particularly for pro-*
fane Swearing.

'Slife , (*that is by God's Life*) Pag. 1,
lin. Antepenult. pag. 23, lin. 35.

Faith.

Faith. Pag. 9, lin. 24.
Pag. 10, lin. 11. and in
twenty other places.

Note, that to prevent Mistakes, the Quotations are taken out of the Fourth Edition, Printed in London, 1704.

In Faith. Pag. 9. lin. 24.
and in seven other places.

Faith and Troth. pag. 6.
lin. 5.

'Sheart, (*that is by God's heart*) Pag. 22.
lin. 28, and 36.

'Sdeath (*that is by God's death*) pag. 33.
lin. 8. with several other Examples too tedious to relate.

This Comedy is scandalous for Cursing.
Pox on't. pag. 61, lin 29.
A Pox confound *&c.* Pag. 3, lin. 5.
pag. 23, lin. 1, pag. 50, lin. 9.
Pox take 'em. pag. 12, lin. 36.
Pox on her. pag. 5. lin. 21 and in seven other Places.
Pox on the Time. Pag. 19, lin. 14.
O damn you Toad. pag. 26. lin. 20.
O hang you. lin. 35.
Devil take you confounded Toad. pag. 27
Oh hang him, old Fox. pag. 57, lin. 1.
The Devil take me. pag. 74, lin. penult.

This Comedy exposeth Marriage; and pleads for Whoring.
You are a Woman now, and must
think

think of a new Man every Morning, and forget him every Night. To marry, is to be a Child again, and play with the same Rattle always. pag. 70, lin. 9. [*Spoken to* Miss Prue *for her Information.*

You have secured your Honour, for you have purchased an Husband which is a perpetual Opportunity for Pleasure; and it is the least I can do to take Care of your Conscience (*that is to lull it asleep*) Pag. 43, lin. 37. [*Note the whole Dialogue is horridly scandalous on this Subject.*

This Comedy exposeth Honour and Conscience.
Honour is a Publick Enemy, and Conscience a Domestick Thief, pag. 43, lin. 32.

This Comedy stinks with lewd and smutty Expressions.

In this respect, *Benjamin* the *Sailor* is such a Monster, that his Words cannot be mentioned at length. His exposing of Marriage, Pag. 35. lin. 39. and pag. 36. lin. 4. is too filthy to be transcribed. He talks Smut, pag. 36, lin. 12 : and *Frail* a Woman answers him in the same Language. His Discourse to *Miss Prue*, pag. 37, lin. 14. is of the same Nature, and his Song, pag. 45, intolerable.

The

The Expreſſion of *Miſs Prue,* pag. 71. lin. 25, will better bear to be tranſcribed, and therefore the Reader ſhall have ſome, though not one half of it, leſt I ſhould tire his Patience or turn his Stomach. *Now my Mind is ſet upon a Man, I will have a Man ſome way or other. Oh! methinks I'm ſick when I think of a Man, and if I cannot have one, I would go to ſleep all my Life.* I ſhall only obſerve that a Father, who puts ſuch Words into the Mouth of his own Daughter, muſt thank himſelf, and acknowledge *God*'s Judgments to be juſt, ſhould he withdraw his Grace and give her up to her own Hearts Luſt, and what is ſpoken for a *Jeſt,* may prove ſo in *Earneſt.*

This Comedy aſperſeth the Government.
Pag. 57, lin. 31, *Foreſight* asks, *Pray what will be done at Court?* To this *Valentine* anſwers, *Scandal* will tell you; I am Truth, I never come there.

Laſtly, *This Comedy is notoriouſly ſcandalous for its profane Ridiculing and Expoſing the Holy Scripture.*
Firſt, As to the *Morality.*
Doth ſhe leave us together out of good Morality? [*To give them an Opportunity for*

for Whoring.] and to do as she would be done by? Pag. 27, lin. 24. [*This is their Interpretation of* Matth. 7. 12. *and thus they pervert the Words of Christ himself, as if he was the Patron of Sin, and commanded us to practise such Uncleanness.*

Thus *Scandal* an *Actor* sollicits Mrs. *Foresight,* she threatens to tell her Husband; he replies, pag. 42. lin. 3. *I'll die a Martyr rather than disclaim my Passion.* Here we have Adultery dignified with the Style of Martyrdom. As if it were as honourable to perish in the Defence of Whoring, as to die for the Cause of Christianity.

Like to this is that of *Angelica* in the End of the Play; *Men are generally Hypocrites and Infidels, they pretend to worship, but have neither Zeal nor Faith: How few like* Valentine *would persevere unto Martyrdom?* Here we have the Language of the *Scriptures,* and the most solemn Instances of Religion prostituted to Courtship and Romance! Here you have a Mistress made God Almighty, adored with Zeal and Faith, and worshipped up to Martyrdom! This, if it were only for the Modesty, is strange Stuff for a Lady to say of her self, and had it not been for the profane Exposing of these Graces, would be far from the *Wit* which some Men pretend they hear in the Play-house. *Se·*

Secondly, *As to the Doctrinal Part.*

Our Blessed Saviour affirms himself *to be the Way, the Truth, and the Light, that he came to bear Witness of the Truth, and that his Word is Truth.* These Expressions are mentioned in this Play to a fine Purpose: For *Valentine* in his pretended Madness tells *Buckram* the Lawyer, pag. 50, lin. 38. pag. 51, lin. 2, 8. pag. 52, lin. 31. *I am Truth.----- I am Truth.----- Who is he that is out of his Way? I am Truth, and can set him right.* Now such Persons as are not pleased with Blasphemy, would never have furnished Frensy with Inspiration, and put our Saviour's Words in the Mouth of a Madman, as if they were both alike.

Pag. 77, lin. 37. *Tattle* would have carried off *Valentine*'s Mistress: But *Valentine* expresseth his Resentment in these Words; Tattle, *I thank you, you would have interposed between me and Heaven, but Providence hath laid Purgatory in your Way.* Thus Heaven is debased into an Amour, made like a Turkish Paradise, and Providence brought in to direct the paultry Concerns of the Stage, as if God delighted to see himself mock'd.

Pag. 22, lin. 32. *Jeremy* saith, *I was born with the same Whoreson Appetites too that*

that my Master speaks of. This is strange
Language to such as consider, that *God*
was the Author of these Inclinations to
Eating and Drinking. The *Manichæans*
who believed that Creation was the Work
of the Devil, could scarcely have been
thus course. And *Julian* the *Apostate* was
never (as I think) so blasphemous as to
load our Blessed Saviour with such an Epi-
thet. [*From such Expressions, Good Lord
deliver us.*]

Pag. 23. lin. 12. *Sir Sampson,* speaking
of the Frame of Human Bodies, rails at
them saying, *These Things are unreasona-
ble,* and then he proceeds with an Oath ;
*Why was not I a Bear, that my Cubs
might have lived by sucking their Paws?
Nature hath been provident only to Bears and
Spiders, the one has its Nutriment in his own
Hand, and the other spins his Habitation
out of his Entrails.* This the Play-house
Paraphrase on the 139th *Psalm* ; and thus
they give God thanks for the Advantage
of their Being.

Thirdly, As to the historical Part.

Pag. 65, lin. 32, Sir *Sampson* saith,
am one of your Patriarchs, I, a Branch o
your Antediluvian *Families, Fellows tha*
the Floud could not wash away. Here th
Scripture

Scripture-Account of the Floud is expofed as falfe, and *God* himfelf made a Lyar to pleafe the Auditors.

Pag. 68, lin. 11. *Sir Sampfon* tells the fine *Angelica*, Sampfon's *a very good Name for an able Fellow : Your* Sampfon's *were ftrong Dogs from the Beginning.*

To this *Angelica* anfwers; *Have a care, and don't over-act your Part. If you remember , the ftrongeft* Sampfon *of your Name pull'd an old Houfe over his Head at laft.* Here we have again the facred Hiftory burlefqu'd, and *Sampfon* once more brought into the Houfe of *Dagon,* to make Sport for the *Plihftins.*

Pag. 40, lin. 25. *There have been wife Men, but they were fuch as you: Men who confulted the Stars, and were obfervers of Omens.* This is a Character of Aftrology, and Heathen Vanities, far different from what we find in Scripture. But that which follows is more profane. Solomon *was wife, but how? by his Judgment in* Aftrology. This was fpoken to *Forefight,* who was, as the *Drama* tells us, *an illiterate old Fellow, pretending to underftand Aftrology, Palmeftry, Phyfiognomy, Omens, Dreams, &c.* Now according to the Language of the Play-houfe, *Solomon* and *Forefight* had their Underftandings qualified alike.

alike. This is the Players Account of Solomon's supernatural Knowledge! Thus
the wiseſt Prince is dwindled into a Gyp-
ſie; and thoſe glorious Gifts of God look'd
on as nothing but Dotage and Erecting of
Schemes.

I am ſick of ſuch horrid, blaſphemous
Language, and ſhall therefore only add
what follows in the ſame Page, lin. 31.
*The Wiſe Men of the Eaſt owed their In-
ſtructions to a Star; which is rightly obſer-
ved by* Gregory *the* Great, *in favour of
Aſtrology.* This was the Star which ſhone
at our Saviour's Birth. Now according
to the Players Language, and the Banter
in the forementioned Page, any one would
conclude they take it to be no more than
an *Ignis Fatuus,* to lead People out of the
Way. And thus while we obſerve the
Feaſt of *Epiphany* they ridicule the Mi-
racle.

There are many ſcandalous Expreſſions
in this Play which I ſhall not relate. But
from hence we may obſerve that the
Church and Play-houſe are as contrary to
each other as *Chriſt* and *Belial,* Light and
Darkneſs, Heaven and Hell. The Deſign
of the Church is to make Men ſerious:
the Deſign of the preſent Comedies is chiefly
to make Men laugh. The Deſign of Religion

ligion is to awaken the Conscience; but the Design of the Stage is to *sear it with an hot Iron*. And therefore (as Mr. *Collier* observes, pag. 96.) *Profaneness, tho' never so well corrected, is not to be endured. It ought to be banished without* Proviso *or* Limitation. *No Pretence of Character or Punishment can excuse it ; or any* Stage-Discipline *make it tolerable.* 'Tis grating *to* Christian *Ears, dishonourable to the Majesty of God, and dangerous in the Example. And in a Word it tends to no Point, unless it be to wear off the Horrour of the Practice, to weaken the Force of Conscience, and to teach the Language of the Damned.*

I shall therefore conclude at present with two Observations, which may fully be proved, and leave the Reader to make his own Inferences from them.

First. In all these Countries where the Patriarchs travailed, and where God appeared either by himself, his Angels, or his Prophets, in order to reveal his Will, and in all those Countries where the *Israelites* sojourned, as well as in the Land of *Canaan* where they afterwards lived, there was no such thing either known, or perhaps so much as talk'd of as a *Publick Stage*: and for this Reason there

there is no Word in the antient *Hebrew* or *Chaldee* Languages to signify either a *Comedy*, or a *Tragedy*. But on the contrary, these Interludes were invented in *Greece*, and confined for many Ages to those Countries, where the Devil generally deluded the People from their Oracles, returned Answers to such as came to enquire of him, and directed them according as he thought most convenient for his own Interest.

Secondly. The *Antient* Design of these Acts, among the *Heathens* (both *Greeks* and *Latins*) was to encourage *Religion* and *Virtue* ; but to expose *Vice* and *Profaneness*. On the contrary, the *present* Design among us who pretend to be *Christians* is to expose *Religion* and *Virtue* ; but to encourage *Vice* and *Profaneness*.

F I N I S.

_____

B R I S T O L, Printed by *W. Bonny* in *Corn-street*. 1705.
_____

A
SERMON

PREACHED in the

PARISH-CHURCH

O F

St. *Butolph*'s *Aldgate*,

I N T H E

CITY of *LONDON*,

O N

Sunday the thirtieth Day of *November*,
In the Year of Our LORD 1729.

Occafioned by the

Erecting of a PLAY-HOUSE

In the Neighbourhood.

Publifhed at the Requeft of feveral of the Auditors.

By *ARTHUR BEDFORD*, M. A.

Chaplain to the Worfhipful the *Haberdafher's Hof-pital* at *Hoxton*, and Preacher of the Afternoon Sermons on Sundays at St. *Butolph*'s *Aldgate*, aforefaid.

LONDON:

Printed by *Charles Ackers* in *Great-Swan-Alley*, St. *John's-Street*; and Sold by J. HOOKE at the *Flower-de-Luce*, overagainft St. *Dunftan*'s Church, in *Fleetftreet*; W. MEADOWS at the *Angel* in *Cornhill*; and T. COX under the *Royal-Exchange*. 1730. (Price Six-Pence.)

TO THE

Worſhipful His MAJESTY's Juſtices of the Peace in and near the Pariſh of *White-chappel*, in the Suburbs of the City of *London*, and in the County of *Middleſex*.

May it pleaſe Your Worſhips,

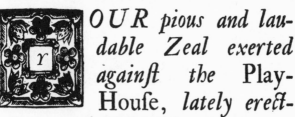OUR *pious and lau-dable Zeal exerted againſt the Play-Houſe, lately erect-ed in your Neighbourhood, en-courages me to dedicate to You what I have done for the ſame End, though in another Manner. And as I doubt not, but Your*

* A   *Endeavours*

DEDICATION.

Endeavours are acceptable both to GOD and all good Men, and even to all those, who cannot be supported in your Neighbourhood, but by Trade and Industry, and who dread the Consequences of Idleness and Extravagancy, especially in these Parts; so if this small Treatise is acceptable to Yourselves, it will be a very great Satisfaction to

Your Worships most Affectionate,

And most Humble Servant,

ARTHUR BEDFORD

2 Tim. ii. 16.

But shun profane and vain bablings; for they will increase unto more ungodliness.

HE Erecting of a *Play-House* in the Neighbourhood obliges me to warn this Congregation of the great Evil and Danger in Frequenting them: So that though there are many Vices in Conversation, which this Text adviseth us to avoid, I shall at present only apply the same to the *publick Actings* of the *Stage* in *Comedies* and *Tragedies,* and other Diversions of the same Nature, and endeavour to shew, That we ought to *shun* those *profane and vain bablings,* since a long Experience doth fully convince us, that *they do increase unto more ungodliness.*

In order to this it may be thought requisite, that I should prove these Diversions to be *profane and vain bablings.* But since this is as evident, as that the Sun shines at Noon-Day, since none in this Age deny it, except Persons of lewd Morals, and a reprobate Sense, I think, the Matter too notorious to be at this Time insisted on, and only desire such, who doubt the Truth hereof, that

A 2   they

they would serioufly perufe *the View of the Immorality and Profaneness of the* English *Stage, with the Sense of Antiquity on this Argument* (a). And alfo a fmaller Treatife, entituled, *A Reprefentation of the Impiety and Immorality of the* English *Stage, with Reafons for Putting a Stop thereto, and fome Queftions addrefs'd to thofe, who frequent the Play-Houfes,* or fome others of thofe many Treatifes which have been fince publifhed on the fame Subjects; in the Perufal of which they may be fully fatisfied, That the Mifbehaviour of the *Stage,* in Refpect to Morality and Religion, is intolerable, and it doth far exceed the Examples of the former, and even of the Heathen Ages and Poets, and the Liberties, which they take, are often offenfive to the Profeffion of *Chriftianity,* which plainly appears from their *lewd and filthy Communication,* their *Swearing, Curfing, Blafphemy, Profanenefs, and lewd Application of Scripture;* their *Abufe of the Clergy,* to make the Religion, which they profefs, vile and contemptible ; and alfo their *Giving great Characters to Libertines,* or Perfons who fcruple no Vice or Immorality, and Bringing them off with Honour and Succefs. How a fine (b) Gentleman is a whoring, fwearing, curfing, fmutty, atheiftical Man. Thefe Qualifications ferve to compleat the Idea of Honour, and are the top Improvements of Fortune, and the diftinguifhing Glories of Birth and Breeding ; and when all this is added to bold and daring Attempts after rich Fortunes, they are rewarded according to their Wifhes, and inftruct the Audience how to carry on the fame Intreagues to the Ruin of other Families. In fhort, their Actions are chiefly defigned

(a) By Jeremiah Collier.   (b) Collier's *View of the Stage,* Page 143.

to gratify such Persons, as are of vicious and debauched Principles, who *fear not* GOD, *and regard not man*; since it is generally from such, that they have their Wealth. Hence it is, that their Poets seldom scruple to speak Blasphemy, rather than lose a Fancy, and to affront their GOD, whilst they adore their Mistress. Hence it is, that they look upon the Regulating the Play-Houses, and Keeping them within the Bounds of Modesty and Religion, to be the greatest Persecution, and which would in the End prove the Suppressing of them. For as they have given a just Scandal to good Men; so if they had not such Acts and Expressions, which will please the bad, they must fall at once, and Necessity will compel them to take other Employments. I shall not therefore spend any Time in Proving these Things to be *profane and vain bablings*, but endeavour to shew you the Reasons which should induce us to avoid them, and especially that which is mentioned in the Text; because, if they are encouraged, *they will increase unto more ungodliness.*

To this End let us first consider *the Precepts* and *Examples of the Primitive Christians.* It is (c) very remarkable, that the *ancient Fathers* have spoken most fully, against the *Plays*, which were used both in *Rome* and *Greece*; and, if we did quote all, which hath been said by them upon this Subject, we must transcribe a great Part of their Works, since they have written particular *Books*, as well as *Homilies* or *Sermons*, upon this Occasion. *Lactantius* (d) wondered at the Practice of the *Heathen Philosophers*, who were present at the Actings of such *publick Interludes*, and saith, That *because*

(c) Collier's *View of the Stage, from Page* 250 *to Page* 276.
(d) Lactantius, *lib.* 6. *cap.* 20.

they

they are the publick Allurements of Vices, and do so effectually prevail to the Corrupting of Men's Minds, they ought to be suppressed; especially because they are not only unprofitable in Bringing us to Heaven, but are also very pernicious in Sending us to Hell. And in *(e)* another Place he asks this Question, *Who would not look upon that Man to be very wanton and wicked, who did suffer such Acts in his own House?* And then he adds, That *there is no Difference, whether we are guilty of Lasciviousness alone at Home, or encourage it by Frequenting the same publickly in the Theater.* St. *Cyprian (f)* saith, That *Adultery is learned, whilst these things are seen; and the chast Matron, who goes to behold such Sights, returns Home with a corrupt and debauched Mind.* Here (saith he) *Wickedness is beheld most willingly and with Delight. What then cannot such Actions persuade others to do?* And therefore he adviseth us to *consider, Whether a Person can be either innocent or modest, who is present at such Things?*

And as the *(g)* Primitive *Christians* did constantly urge the Necessity of Abstaining from these *Plays*; so such, as owned themselves *Christians*, did as conscientously follow their Advice. They went not to the publick *Games*, nor frequented the *Shows*, which were made for the Diversion and Entertainment of the People; and this was so publickly known that the Heathens charged it upon them as a Crime. *Cæcilius* in *Minutius Fælix* (h) complains thus, *That the Romans governed and enjoyed the World, whilst the* Christians *in the mean time were careful and mopish. They abstained from*

(e) Lactantius, *lib.* 6. *cap.* 21.   *(f)* Cyprianus *in Epistolâ ad Donatum.*   *(g)* Dr. Cave's *Primitive Christianity,* Book 2. *Chap.* 2. *Page* 32.   *(h)* *Pag.* 34, Oxford *Edition.*

such

such Pleasures, they visited not the Shows, nor were present at the Pomps. They frequented not the publick Feasts, but abhorred all such Diversions. This *Octavius,* the *Christian,* granted to be *true,* when he pleaded their Defence, and said in Answer to this Charge, That (*i*) *since they were endued with Modesty and Sobriety, they had just Cause to abstain from those evil Pleasures, their Pomps and Shows, and to condemn them as hurtful Allurements.* And he gives this Reason, *because in those Acts and scenical Representations their filthy Communication is as great as their Madness, whilst the Actors speaking of Adulteries incite them, and the Stage-Players by Describing of Lust do inflame their Hearers.* In short, (*k*) they thought, they could not be present at these Plays without great Sin and Shame, without Affronting their Modesty, and Offering a Distaste and Horrour to their Minds. They look'd upon the publick Sports and Pastimes of those Days, as the Scenes not only of Folly and Lewdness, but of great Impiety and Idolatry, as Places where the Devil eminently ruled, and reckoned those to be his Votaries, who went thither.

And as they thought it a great Crime to be present at such Sports ; so they looked upon it as contrary to their *Baptismal Vow.* At the Time when Persons were baptized, they were (*l*) among others asked these two Questions, *Dost thou renounce the Devil, and all his Works, Powers, and Services? And dost thou renounce the World, and all its Pomps and Pleasures?* And to each of these Questions the Party answered, saying, *I do renounce them.* And each of these Questions they supposed to be directly levelled against the Thea-

---

(*i*) *Page* 106.   (*k*) Dr. Cave's *Primitive Christianity, Part* 2.
Chap. 2. *Page* 32.   (*l*) Constitutiones Apostolicæ, *lib.* 7.
cap. 42. *pag.* 993.

ters.

ters. St. *Cyril* (*m*) expounding the Word-*Pomps*
(the Word which we still use in our Baptism, in a
Question of the same Nature) expresly tells us,
that thereby is meant *The Sights and Sports of the
publick Stage.* Those (*n*) *pompous Spectacles, Plays,
and scenical Representations* exhibited in the *Roman*
and *Grecian Theaters,* which, because they were
so lewd, cruel, and impious, it was an early Cus-
tom for the *primitive Bishops* and *Fathers* of the
Church, in their Discourses to the *baptized Persons,*
strictly to enjoin them not to frequent, or so much
as once to be present or seen at such Places.
They reckoned (*o*) all those *Pomps* as *Allurements*
to *Vice,* and those *Houses* as so many *Synagogues* of
Satan, and consequently, that by *Renouncing the
World and the Devil* they also renounced them. Accordingly *Tertullian* tells us (*p*) of a *Christian Woman, who, going to the Theater, was there possessed
by the Devil; and when the evil Spirit at his
Casting out was asked, How he durst set upon a
Christian?* he *presently answered, I did but what
was fit and just, for I found her upon my own
Ground.* Neither is this the only Instance, which

<hr />

(*m*) Cyrillus Hierosolym. *Catech. Myst: Vol.* 1. *Page* 510.
(*n*) *Dr.* Bray *on the Church-Catechism, Sect.* 19.   (*o*) *It may
may be observed from* St. Cyril, *that the Word* Pompa *is used to
signify the* Acts *of the* Stage, *tho' that is not its only Meaning.
It may also be observed, that the Word was used in this Sense both
by* Heathens *and* Christians. *The* Heathen *in* Minutius Fælix
charged the Christians *with this pretended Crime,* Non Pompis in-
tereftis; *and the* Christians *confessed the Charge, saying,* meritò
malis voluptatibus, & Pompis veftris, & Spectaculis abftinemus.
And therefore as the Word Pomps *is expresly used in our Renunciation at* Baptism, *and in our Church-Catechism; as also we ratify
and confirm the same in our own Persons at Confirmation, and as the
Word is of a* Greek Original; *so, I think, that there is Reason to
take it according to the Sense of a* Greek *Father, and not confine it
only to the Sense, in which the* Latins *often used it.*   (*p*) *Lib.
de* Spectaculis, *Page* 701. *Edit. Basil* 1562.

he

he there mentions, but he faith, that *there are other Examples of thofe, who, while they held Communion with the Devil by Frequenting thofe Shows, did at the fame Time fall away from the Faith.* And then he adds, *For no Man can ferve two Mafters. What Communion hath Light with Darknefs? And what Fellowfhip hath Life with Death? We ought* (faith he) *to hate thofe Meetings and Affemblies of the Heathen, becaufe there the Name of* GOD *is blafphemed.* And after this he expoftulates thus with thofe in his Time, *Do you doubt but that in the Minute, in which you fhall be prefent at the Synagogue of Satan, all the Angels do look down from Heaven, and behold every one who fpeaks the Blafphemy, and who hears it, who lends a Tongue, and who lends an Ear to the Devil to be employed againft* GOD? *Will you not therefore avoid that Seat of the Enemies of* CHRIST, *that infectious Chair, and that Air, which is polluted with fuch wicked and profane Difcourfe?* And therefore fince our *modern Plays,* which are acted in thofe Houfes, are no lefs inferiour to the *ancient* Ones in *Impiety* and *Lewdnefs* than they are in *Show* and *Pomp*; we may fuppofe, that thofe *ancient Fathers,* if they had lived in our Days, would have expreffed their Refentments now, in the fame Language which they did then. Since they have fuch a malignant Influence upon Faith and Manners, (as it is owned almoft by all Perfons, and as it is generally complained that they have) they may be reckoned among the Works of the *Devil,* as well as thofe of former Ages, and therefore ought not to be encouraged by fuch, who call themfelves *Chriftians.* And fince we alfo have been *baptized,* and have promifed to *Renounce the Devil and all his Works,* as well as *the vain Pomps and Vanities of this wicked World, and all the finful Lufts of the Flefh,* fo

B　　　　　　　　　　*that*

that we will not follow, nor be led by them ; we ought, as they did, to confider the Nature of our *Baptifmal Vow*, and (*q*) beware, left we break that *Covenant*, which we fo folemnly made *with our* GOD.

That this is our prefent Cafe may be abundantly feen in many Books and Treatifes, which have been printed on this Subject; among which I fhall only mention one of the greateft Rank among us, which is Archbifhop *Tillotfon*, who in (*r*) one *Sermon* calls the *Play-Houfe* the *Devil's Chapel*, and *the School and Nurfery of Lewdnefs and Vice*. And in another (*s*) he faith, that *the Plays do intrench upon natural Modefty, and for that Reafon are forbidden and condemned by the Chriftian Religion* ; *and (as they are now ordered among us) are a mighty Reproach to the Age and Nation. That they are intolerable, and not fit to be permitted in a civilized, much lefs in a* Chriftian *Nation, and that they do moft notorioufly minifter both to Infidelity and Vice. By the Profanenefs of them they are apt to inftil bad Principles into the Minds of Men, and to leffen that Awe and Reverence, which all Men ought to have for GOD and Religion. And by their Lewdnefs they teach Vice, and are apt to infect the Minds of Men, and difpofe them to lewd and diffolute Practices. And therefore* (as he adds) *I do not fee how any Perfon, pretending to Sobriety and Virtue, and efpecially to the pure and holy Religion of our bleffed SAVIOUR, can without great Guilt, and open Contradiction to his holy Profeffion, be prefent at fuch lewd and immodeft Plays, much lefs frequent them, as too many do, who yet would take it very ill to be*

(*q*) Prov. ii. 17.   (*r*) *In his third Sermon concerning the Education of Children, Page* 220. *Firft Edition.*   (*s*) *Vol.* 11, *Page* 319, 320, 321.

fhut

shut out of the Communion of Christians ; *as they would most certainly have been in the first and purest Ages of* Christianity.

And now let us consider the Reason, which the *Apostle* urgeth in the Text. If we should encourage this Evil, it will make Way for more : And, if we do not *shun these profane and vain bablings, they will increase unto more ungodliness.* In vain do we pretend to a *Reformation of Manners* and a *Regulation of our Youth,* when such Temptations lie in their Way, which, if frequented, will certainly debauch them. In this Case we must expect that Youth will follow what is most agreeable to their corrupt Inclinations ; and whilst the Temptations are equally strong on either Side, and the Heart of Man is fully set in him to do Evil, we cannot but expect, that the Consequences hereof will be fatal to some, and that the *Devil* will not be wanting to make Use of such Opportunities to tempt Men to Sin, until they are involved in eternal Destruction. The sad Experience hereof made *Menander,* a Heathen *Poet,* to say, That *evil Communications do corrupt good Manners* ; which was so certain and true, that it became a *Proverb* in *Greece,* and was afterward assented to by St. *Paul,* who inserts the same into the *holy Scriptures* with a particular Caution of his own, lest we should be deceived by such Insinuations. And therefore it may not be amiss to suppose, that St. *Paul,* directing his Epistle to *Timothy* at *Ephesus,* where the *Comedies* of *Aristophanes* were frequently acted, might have a particular Reference to these Enormities, when he advised him to *shun profane and vain bablings,* because *they* would *increase unto more ungodliness :* And indeed we there find the Effects thereof, for *(t)* their Manners were *loose* and *pro-*

(*t*) Strabo *Geogr. lib.* 14. *pag.* 41.

B 2   *fligate.*

fligate, wanton, and *effeminate*; and they had an Injunction in their common Difcourfe, *Let none of
ours be thrifty.* And if this was the Cafe in a City,
where they could hardly be worfe, what Degene-
racy muft be expected in a Place profeffing *Chriftianity,* and making, at leaft, fome Show of Religion?

But it is not fufficient to fpeak of the Increafe
of Ungodlinefs in general ; and therefore I' fhall
mention fome particular Vices, which feem, in a
great Meafure, to be the Effects of our prefent
Stage and their Actings.

The firft is, The Profaning of GOD's Name
by *Swearing, Curfing,* and *Blafphemy.* The Increafe of this Vice is moft amazing, and no one
that walks the Streets is fure, that he fhall not
hear People calling upon GOD to *damn* and *confound,* fometimes themfelves, and fometimes others,
and more particularly that the *Plague* may rot
them. There are innumerable and intolerable Examples of thefe Sorts in our modern Plays, as they
have been fully expofed by later Authors ; and
thefe are fpoken as Patterns for the *Bullies* of the
Age to imitate. The Difappointments in *Comedies* are never thought to be fufficiently exprefs'd,
nor the Paffions in *Tragedies* to be fufficiently rais'd,
until their Refentments are mixed with fuch hellifh
Language. Neither are they contented with fuch
as are more common, becaufe it looks as if they had
not Wit enough to affront GOD more effectually than their Neighbours ; but they are daily
inventing a continual Variety of this Nature, as
if the *Play-Houfe* was only a Forge to hammer out
new Pieces of Armour, whereby to rebel againft
GOD, and bid him Defiance. They who hear
them with Delight foon learn them, and afterward ufe
them in other Places ; and thus like Perfons fick
of

of the Plague (which they often call for) they carry the Infection from Place to. Place, and so it overspreads the Nation.

Secondly, *Murthers* are often the Effects of the *Stage.* Many of our modern *Tragedies* are designed to shew the Success of such, who think their Wills to be a Law, who hector at, quarrel with, fight and destroy all before them. To these it is that the Actors pay Respect, give them great Titles, admire their Courage, and praise their Vices, instead of Virtues. Such Sights, Bloodshed, and Murther, being shewn on a Stage, do by Degrees occasion the Spectators to be cruel and outrageous; and Men do there learn to be *inhuman.* Such Persons, who are in the Heat of Youth, and are of a proud and passionate Temper, immediately think, that they may act the same Parts upon the publick Stage of the World, and come off with the same Success, until they are convinced of their Error, when perhaps it is too late. And it is very observable, that the greatest Persecutions, which were ever raised against the *Christians,* were began and carried on in *Heathen Rome,* where they had their *Theaters,* and their *Tragedies* were most frequently acted. This made them more cruel and delight in Bloodshed, insomuch that, at last, the Martyrdom of the Saints became their Diversion, and *Christians* were in Reality brought forth, and devoured by wild Beasts, to make Pastime for those, who had pleased themselves with such Resemblances. And since the Reformation it is as remarkable, that the most dreadful Persecutions against the Protestants, and all their Designs to destroy our Religion, have either been begun, or, at least, carried on and promoted by that City. This is the *great Whore,* who hath been diverted by the *Theaters, Carnivals* and *Jubilees;*

bilees ; and, as fhe was addicted to fuch Sports and
Paftimes, it may be the lefs wondered at, that
in all Ages fhe hath made herfelf fo *drunk with
the Blood of the Saints.* And even, among our-
felves, it will be difficult to find one Inftance of a
Challenge or a Duel, except among fuch, whofe
Spirits have been warmed by being prefent at fuch
a Furnace as this. But, having feen fuch Things
in jeft, they lofe their Lives in earneft.

Thirdly, Adulteries and *Whoredoms* are the common Effects of the *Stage.* In one of our *Plays*
(*u*) an Actor boafts, that this Effect is fo vifible
in their Neighbourhood, that their Hearers cannot fail of Opportunities for fuch a Purpofe. And
indeed the notorious Immodefty, both in Words
and Actions, which are there both heard and feen,
the filthy Songs which are there fung, and the
Mufick framed by the Compofers with fuch Notes,
as will moft affect the Paffions, are but as fo many
Temptations to Luft, and ferve only to inftruct
the Hearers, how to carry on their own filthy
Defigns, that fo, at their Departure thence in a
mix'd Company, they may go (if poffible) to a
worfe Place, and be the real Actors of what was
thus reprefented. Neither do the Effects ftop here.
Thefe Songs are taught to young Ladies to fing,
before they are fenfible what they mean, and fo
the Parents pay for the Ruin of their own Children. Thus they learn Love-Songs, and fuch as are
frequently intermix'd with Smut, and even Mo-
tives to Luft : Thefe they are obliged frequently
to repeat, before they can learn them, and the
Mufician feldom fails to fet the worft Part off to

(*u*) Gibraltar, *Page* 6. *Line* 9. *Whores* are dog-cheap here in
London. For a Man may ftep into the *Play-Houfe* Paffage, and
pick up Half-a-dozen for Half-a-crown.

the greatest Advantage ; sometimes by a frequent
Repetition of the Words, sometimes by Affecting
Divisions, and always by such soft Notes, which,
they too well know, will work upon that Passion.
This of course makes them wanton, and so they
think of Husbands, before they are capable
to choose for themselves. Thus they are soon en-
snared to gratify their Passions, by others who only catch at their Fortunes ; and are often tempted to worse Acts, which prove the Ruin of themselves, and the Sorrow of their Parents. Thus
our noble Science of Musick is debased, and, like
Cannon taken by the Enemy, is directly levelled
against the first Proprietor. It was, at first, intended in the Church of GOD to set forth his
Glory both in publick and private, and be a Help
to us in our Way to Heaven ; but, instead of this
ancient Design, it is abused to his Dishonour, and
there is very little private Use made of it, unless it is to debauch Men's Morals, to heighten
their Lusts, and send them directly into the
Road to Hell. Good Men may wish, and pray,
and endeavour for a Regulation ; but it must be
an over-ruling Providence which can effect it,
and to him alone in such a Case must the Glory be
given.

Fourthly, Idleness is the common Effect of the
Stage. It is with great Difficulty, that Youth are
kept to Labour and Industry ; and therefore all
Temptations to the contrary are prejudicial. But,
when such leave their Callings to go to the Plays,
it is but seldom, that the Masters have any Command of those who are under them. They have
a strange Inclination to go thither again and again ;
and so all necessary Business shall be neglected to
gratify their Fancy. Besides, it is usually late,
before the *Plays* are ended, and, if the Company

is large, the Heat of the Place will make them thirſty. This expoſeth them to go to *Taverns* and *Alehouſes*, and then it is ſo much the later, before they return Home. By this Means Families are diſordered, and forced to keep unſeaſonable Hours, and therefore they cannot be ſo early about their lawful Callings. After this, ſuch Youth think themſelves too good to be confined, and grow weary of the Station, in which GOD hath placed them. Thus the Principles of Idleneſs and Extravagancy are ſtrangely infuſed into ſuch People, as reſort to theſe Places, which often tend to their utter Ruin. This may be an Argument to perſuade all Tradeſ-men and Shopkeepers to reſtrain their Children, Servants, and Apprentices. If they are ſuffered to go thither, they will be apt to frequent them ; and, if they have no Money of their own for ſuch a Purpoſe, they will be apt, as Occaſion requires, to ſteal it from their Parents and Maſters, which being done by little and little, it may be long before it is miſſed in the Way of Trade, and after that it will be impoſſible to know how much they have been injured.

Fifthly, *Contempt of all Religion* is too often the Effect of the Stage. As ſuch Perſons ſeldom ſcruple to ſpeak the moſt horrid Blaſphemies, as a Diverſion and Entertainment to their Company ; ſo we cannot expect, that they, who are delighted with ſuch Things, can be reckoned Men, who have any Senſe of the Honour of GOD, or Fear of his Judg-ments. Nothing is more common here for ſuch, than to affront their Maker, and make a Goddeſs of their Miſtreſs, to think of no Heaven, except in her Company, and no Hell, but to be kept from her. This and much more, which one would tremble to relate, is the Language of the Play-Houſe, and indeed ſome of the beſt. An Author

in

in the latter End (*x*) of the laſt Century, ſpeaking of this (*y*) Subject, quotes out of the printed Plays, then extant, ſeveral Examples, where
(*z*) the Service of GOD in a Church and Prayer is ridiculed, where they (*a*) ſwear by *Mahomet*, (*b*) contemn even Heaven itſelf, and (*c*) give
the Preference to a *Turkiſh* Paradiſe; where (*d*)
they make a Jeſt of their *Baptiſmal Vow*, where
(*e*) they look upon *Providence* to be a ridiculous
Superſtition, and affirm, (*f*) that none but Blockheads pretend to Religion. In one of their Plays,
(*g*) like *Lucian* and *Celſus*, they deride the Reſurrection. One (*h*) ſpeaks againſt the Immortality
of the Soul, and (*i*) another brings in a *lewd Italian* Proverb for Authority, in Contempt of the
holy Scriptures. All this was in the Infancy of
this Impiety, which is now grown up to a Mon-
ſter. Since this we have had the *Devil* (*k*) directly
owned as a GOD, in Defiance of the firſt Commandment, he is called (*l*) a *more than mortal
Power*; and the Inference is, that it is a *Raſh-
neſs* and *Folly* to reſiſt him, not without a profane
Alluſion to that Text of *Scripture*, (*m*) *Thou ſhalt
not tempt the LORD thy GOD*. Here we have

(*x*) A ſhort View of the Profaneneſs and Immorality of the
Engliſh Stage, *by* Jeremiah Collier; *the firſt Edition whereof was
about the Year* 1686. (*y*) A ſhort View of the Stage, *Chap.* 2.
Page 56, &c. (*z*) Page 66. (*a*) Page 61. (*b*) Page 81.
(*c*) Page 61. (*d*) Page 63. (*e*) Page 81. (*f*) Page 78, *and*
147. (*g*) Page 66. (*h*) Page 68. (*i*) Page 67. (*k*) *Thus
an Actor ſpeaks to the Devil in the* Britiſh Enchanters, *in order to
gratify his private Revenge. Page* 12. *Line* 22.

See it perform'd———and thou ſhalt be,
Dire Inſtrument of Hell, a God to me.

(*l*) The Britiſh Enchanters, *Page* 16. *Line* 2.
Forbear, raſh Mortal, give thy Frenzy o'er
For now thou tempt'ſt a more than mortal Power.
(*m*) Deut. vi. 16. Matth. iv. 7.

C   the

the (*n*) *Eternity*, the *Omniprefence*, the *Wifdom*
and *Knowledge*, the *Goodnefs*, the *Truth*, and
the *Vengeance* of GOD, in plain *Englifh*, attributed to the *Devil*. Accordingly he is frequently pray'd to, and mentioned inftead of GOD, in
their ferious Ejaculations. In one (*o*) *Comedy*
there is a Song directly in Praife of the *Devil*,
and the (*p*) Salutation of *our* SAVIOUR to his
Apoftles after his Refurrection, and of (*q*) the Angel to the *Virgin Mary*, is not only in (*r*) another Place put into the Mouth of a Witch ; but
here it is given as a Compliment to thefe *Powers be-
neath*, who are there reprefented as altering the
divine Decrees ; and it is farther added, that the
Actors, wherever they come, do in this Manner
provoke the Divine Juftice, and dare even the

GOD

(*n*) *See the Book intituled,* A ferious Remonftrance in Behalf of
the Chriftian Religion, againft the horrid Blafphemies and Impieties, which are ftill ufed in the *Englifh* Play-Houfes, to the great
Difhonour of Almighty GOD, and in Contempt of the Statutes
of this Realm, *particularly Chap.* 7. *or*, The Divine Attributes
afcribed to the Devil on the Stage, *Page* 76 *to Page* 90. (*o*) The
Metamorphofis, *Page* 14.

> Hail, Powers beneath, whofe Influence imparts
> The Knowledge of infernal Arts ;
> By whofe unerring Gifts we move
> To alter the Decrees above,
> Whether on Earth, or Seas, or Air,
> The mighty Miracle we dare.

That is, Wherever the Actors come, they fet the great GOD *of
Heaven at Defiance, provoke him to enter into Judgment, and even
dare him to do his worft. This is but the third Part of the Song,
which concludes with invoking the Help, and craving the Affiftance
of thefe infernal Powers ; but I fuppofe that the Reader doth not defire
that I fhould tranfcribe any more, fince, if* GOD *fhould enter into
Judgment, all the Blood of the Nation is not fufficient to atone for
this.* (*p*) Matth. xxviii. 9. (*q*) Luke i. 28. (*r*) Mackbeth, *Page* 4. *Line* 34, 35, 36. *and Page* 5. *Line* 9, 10, 11, 15.
The Word is Hail, *which is now grown obfolete and out of Ufe, and
others*

GOD of Heaven to do his worft. ۱ In *(s)* a late Play, frequently acted, the *Devil* is exprefly faid to be *a very modeft Perfon*, with other Expreffions, too vile to be mentioned in this Place. In the *Old Teftament* we are ftrictly charged *(t)* not to *fuffer a witch to live*, and in the *New (u) Witchcraft* is mentioned as *the works of the flefh*, and that *they, who do fuch things, cannot inherit the kingdom of* GOD. In a *Play*, very frequently acted at this Time, we have *(x) Mufick*, and (y) *Songs*, and *(z) Dances* for *Witches*; they enter (a) flying upon the *Stage*, and (b) go off again in the fame Manner, and *(c)* a whole Train of Witchcraft is imitated. In their Difcourfe *(d)* they talk of commanding the Winds, and making foul Weather to the Diftrefs of Mariners, and Revenge of themfelves. In one of their Songs they give us an Account *(e)* of their merry Way of Living, and that *(f) all Things go fair for their Delight*; and after that *(g)* they folemnly commend *Witchcraft*, in a large Song for that Pur-

pofe.

---

others are come up inftead of it; *fo that on our prefent Stage, it hath neither Wit nor Senfe, but as it is a profane Burlefquing of the* facred Scriptures. *(s)* The Recruiting Officer, *Page* 50. *Line* 32. Look ye, fair Lady, the Devil is a very modeft Perfon, he feeks no Body, unlefs they feek him firft; befides, he is chain'd up like a Maftiff, and cannot ftir, unlefs he is let loofe. *This Expreffion makes the Petition very impertinent, which* Our SAVIOUR *hath commanded us to ufe,* Lead us not into temptation, but deliver us from the evil; *and gives the Lie to the Expreffion of St.* Peter, 1 Epift. v. 8., Be fober, be vigilant; becaufe your adverfary the devil, as a roaring lion, walketh about feeking whom he may devour.. *(t)* Exod. xxii. 18. *(u)* Gal. v. 19, 20. *(x)* Mackbeth, *Page* 39. *l.* 38. *and p.* 44. *l.* 9. *(y)* Ibid. *p.* 24. *l.* 32. *p.* 25. *l.* 19. *p.* 39. *l.* 38. *p.* 40. *l.* 1, 17 *and* 23. *(z)* Ibid. *p.* 25. *l.* 19. *p.* 26. *l.* 6. *and p.* 44. *l.* 9. *(a)* Ibid. *p.* 3. *l.* 22. *(b) Page* 1. *l.* 14. *(c)* Ibid. *p.* 41, &c. *Act* 4. *Scene* 1. *(d)* Ibid. *p.* 3. *l.* 23. *(e)* Ibid. *p.* 25. *l.* 19. *(f)* Ibid. *p.* 40. *l.* 18. *(g)* Ibid. *p.* 40. *l.* 23. Oh, pofe. From this *Play* we may fee what Freedom they take on all Occafions with the *facred Scriptures*. In thefe Books we are told, *(h)* that it is the *glorious GOD*, who *makes a decree for the rain, and a way for the lightning and the thunder*, and *(i) brings the winds out of his treafures*. Here we have thefe Things reprefented as *(k)* raifed by *Devils*, and alfo *(l)* by *Witches*, and their Diverting themfelves at fuch a Time. The *Scriptures*, fpeaking of the Glory of GOD, fay, *(m)* That *he maketh the clouds his chariot, and walketh upon the wings of the wind*. And a like Expreffion is ufed by an Actrefs on the Stage,

> Oh, what a dainty Pleafure's this,
> To fail i'th' Air,
> Whilft the Moon fhines fair,
> To fing, to toy, to dance, and kifs !
> Over Woods, high Rocks, and Mountains,
> Over Hills, and mighty Fountains,
> Over Steeples, Towers, and Turrets
> We fly by Night 'mongft Troops of Spirits.
> No Rings of Bells to our Ears founds ;
> No Howls of Wolves nor Yelps of Hounds :
> No nor the Noife of Water's Breach,
> Nor Cannons Throats our Heights can reach.

From all the deceits of the world, the flefh, and the devil, Good LORD deliver us.   *(h)* Job xxviii. 26. Pfal. xviii. 11, 12, 13, 14. Pfal. xxix. 3.   *(i)* Pfal. cxxxv. 7.   *(k)* Rinaldo, *p.* 45. *l.* 23. The Britifh Enchanters, *p.* 16. *l.* 19. *p.* 33. *l. penult, and p.* 34. *l.* 8.   *(l)* Mackbeth, *p.* 1. *Act* 1. *Scene* 1, *and p.* 3. *l.* 21. *Where Showers are added, and the Witches fpeak thus one to another,*

> When fhall we three meet again,
> In Lightning, Thunder, and in Rain.

(m) Pfal. civ. 3.

when

when she speaks of *(n)* the Devil sitting in a foggy Cloud at the same Time. And to add but one Instance more, The *(o)* Words of the LORD, *sitting upon his throne*, are put into *(p)* the Mouth of the *Devil*, that he may vie with him upon the like Occasion, when he speaks to his Witches, as the blessed GOD did to his holy Angels. In short, we have Reason to believe, that the constant Ridiculing, Burlesquing, and Exposing the *sacred Scriptures* with such a general Approbation from the Audience, is a great Reason of the Infidelity of the present Age ; and hath made others so bold, as to treat the Prophecies of the *Old Testament*, and the Miracles of *Our* SAVIOUR in the *New*, with such Scorn and Contempt, and as Cheats and Impostors, the like whereof cannot be met with since the Creation of the World: For he, who

(n) Mackbeth, *Pag.* 39. *line penult.*

> Hark ! I am call'd, my little Spirit (see)
> Sits in a foggy Cloud, and stays for me.

(o). The Prophet Micaiah *describes the Majesty of* GOD *in this Manner*, 1 Kings xxii. 19, 20, 21, 22. I saw the LORD sitting on his throne, and all the host of heaven standing by him on his right hand and on his left. And the LORD said, Who shall persuade Ahab, that he may go and fall at Ramoth Gilead ? And there came forth a spirit and stood before the LORD, and said, I will persuade him. And the LORD said unto him, Wherewith ? And he saith, I will go forth, and I will be a lying spirit in the mouth of all his prophets. And he said, Thou shalt persuade him, and prevail also. Go forth, and do so.　*(p) In* Mackbeth, *Page* 38. *Line* 34. *the Devil thus speaks to his Witches.*

> ———I shall, e're Night,
> Raise from the Center such a Spright,
> As by the Strength of his Illusion
> Shall draw *Mackbeth* to his Confusion.

For the same Purpose, they utter three ambiguous Prophecies to make him bold, Page 43. Line 6, 9, and 17, *which, being taken in a wrong Sense, was the Cause of his Destruction, and added a greater Reputation*

who will read but a few Pages in thefe printed Books, may foon perceive, that they are the per-fect Imitators of the *Play-Houfe* Language.

Laftly, It is a Queftion, how far the *Stage* hath en-couraged even the frequent Robberies on the Roads, and in the Streets. There is fomething new and furprizing, which offers it-felf on this Head. In a late *Play*, which hath had a prodigious Run, to the Scandal of this Nation, we have a *(q) Crew of Beggars*, made fo by their own Vices and Extrava-gancies. The Women, without any Senfe of Decency, own themfelves to be common *(r)* Whores, and feem to *glory in their fhame*; and, to fupply their Neceffi-ties, they take to *(s)* Picking of *Pockets* and Shop-lifting, and *(t)* the Men are for *Robbing* on the Highway. Here we have *(u)* Methods chalked out to train up Perfons to Stealing. Here we have *(x) Picking of Pockets* encouraged, Highway Robberies pleaded for both in *(y) Profe* and *(z)* in *Verfe*, with *(a)* Methods for Intelligence, and *(b)* Murders allowed in fuch Cafes. Here we have alfo a *(c)* Toleration for Going off with the Goods of the honeft Tradefman. Here the Laws, which are made in fuch Cafes, are *(d)* expofed. Here we have *(e)* the *Courtiers*, and *(f) Court Ladies*

Reputation to the Oracles of the Devil, *See* Page 59. Line 25. *for the two firft, and* Line 17. *for the other.*

From the crafts and affaults of the devil, from thy wrath and from everlafting damnation,
    Good LORD deliver us.

(q) The Beggars Opera *Drama.*   *(r) Page* 30. *line* 26, *and* 30. *p.* 31. *l.* 7, 12, 19, 21 *and* 23.   *(s) Page* 29 *and* 30. *(t) Page* 24, 25 *and* 26.   *(u) Page* 2. *line* 31; *and p.* 9. *l.* 7. *(x) Page* 8. *line* 13. *p.* 30. *l.* 15.   *(y) Page* 24, *throughout.* *(z) Page* 26. *l.* 31.   *(a) Page* 25. *l.* 17.   *(b) Page* 5. *l.* 14 *and* 22.   *(c) Page* 30. *l.* 1, 5, 8.   *(d) Page* 24. *l.* 17. *(e) Page* 21. *l.* 11. *p.* 24. *l.* 27. *p.* 53. *l. penult. p.* 54. *l.* 2. *p.* 68. *l.*12. *p.*72. *l.*5. *and p.* 74. *l.* antepenult.   *(f) Page* 9. *line* 35. *p.* 28. *l.* 30, *and p.* 29. *l. antepenult.*

                                         (g) States-

(g) *States-Men* (h) *Lords,* (i) *Gentlemen,* and (k)
Lawyers, treated with the utmost Scorn and Contempt, for no other visible Reason, but because
they desire to be secure in the Possession of
their own, and are therefore willing to put the
Laws in Execution against such Practices as these.
Here we have (l) a Thief-Advocate, who acts
both against Rogues and for them; that is, (m)
he receives stolen Goods, and (n) disposes of
them, both at Home and Abroad, and (o) sometimes to the right Owners. His Business is to
teach them how (p) to plead, to (q) encourage
Cheats, to (r) soften the Evidence, (s) to sink
them, or (t) nail up their Lips, as (u) in his
Power. This he doth, when the Person (as he
calls it) is (x) active and industrious, and to save
them from Transportation, because he can get
more by their Stay at Home. He hates (y)
a lazy Rogue (as he calls him) he (*) saves the
worst, condemns (z) such as he hath the least
Profit by; such who dispose (a) of stolen Goods
without his Knowledge, and especially those who
would live honest. He hath (b) a large Book
of Accompts before him, and (c) his Daughter
is a very considerable Fortune. The principal
Actor is (d) the Captain of a Gang of High-
waymen, with these he meets at a Tavern; there
are eight by Name, and others which are name-

(g) *Page* 1. *l.* 12. *p.* 38. *l.* 5, 12, *and* 18.   (h) *Page* 6. *l.*
11. *p.* 11. *l. ult.*   (i) *Page* 6. *l.* 11. *p.* 15. *l.* 12.   (k)
Page 15. *l.* 22. *p.* 16. *l.* 6. *p.* 21. *l.* 11, *and p.* 31. *l.* 31.   (l)
Page 1. *l. ult.*   (m) *Page* 16. *l.* 11.   (n) *Page* 7. *l.* 23. *p.*
55. *l.* 24, *and p.* 57. *l.* 16.   (o) *Page* 14. *l.* 24, *and p.* 39. *l.*
23.   (p) *Page* 2.   (q) *Page* 2. *l.* 1.   (r) *Page* 2. *l.* 10.
(s) *Page* 66. *l. penult.*   (t) *Page* 68. *l.* 6.   (u) *Page* 67. *l.*
penult.   (x) *Page* 4. *l.* 1.   (y) *Page* 3. *l. penult.*   (*) *Page* 4. *l.* 1.
(z) *Page* 4. *l.* 22.   (a) *Page* 4. *l.* 10, *and* 16.   (b) *Page* 1. *l.* 1.
(c) *Page* 12. *l.* 8.   (d) *Page* 24.

less,

leſs. Here they plead for their Practice, and encourage each other with the utmoſt Encomiums.
This Actor hath *(e)* two Wives at a time, at
leaſt in all outward Appearance. He hath *(f)*
eight Whores with him at once in the Tavern,
and *(g)* and four Women more follow him with
a Child a-piece. This is the Reaſon, that *(h) Marriage* is ſo frequently ridiculed, as alſo *(i)* con-
jugal Affection in a married State; and Adultery,
Whoredom, Polygamy, and Intriguing with Women are ſo frequently pleaded for, both in Proſe
and Verſe, according to the conſtant Practice of
our modern *Comedies.* The Captain of the High-
waymen declares himſelf a common *(k)* Whore-
monger. For his Robberies he is committed to
Newgate, which for this Reaſon is made *(l)* a
Scene on the Stage, and treated as a Jeſt rather
than a real Puniſhment. Here we have *(m)* a
Dance of Priſoners in Chains. Here we have
(n) Plots for Eſcape, drawn up to Perfection for
the Encouragement of ſuch, who like theſe Courſes.
Here we have a *(o)* Scene of Drunkenneſs to
allay the Fears of an Execution. In this the
(p) Villain places all his Hopes; Adds to this, that
he and *(q)* others alſo ridicule and burleſque

(e) Viz. Polly Peachum, *the Daughter to the Thief-Advocate,*
and Lucy *the Daughter of* Lockit, *the Keeper of* Newgate.
(f) Page 28. *l.* 15.   *(g) Page* 74. *l.* 12.   *(h) Page* 7. *l.* 1.
p. 10. *l.* 3. *p.* 11. *l.* 23. *p.* 14. *l.* 8. *p.* 15. *l.* 8. *p.* 16. *l.* 33. *p.*
17. *l.* 21. *p.* 37. *l.* 3. *p.* 39. *l.* 36. *p.* 40. *l.* 7. *p.* 42. *l.* 26. *p.*
61. *l.* 22.   *(i) Page* 18. *l.* 9, *and p.* 34. *l.* 28.   *(k) Page* 27.
l. 11. *with a Song in Praiſe of it, l.* 18. *ſo alſo p.* 29. *l.* 10. *p.* 30.
l. 30, *and p.* 43. *l.* 16.   *(l) Page* 49. *l.* 2.   *(m) Page* 70. *l.* 4.
(n) Page 41. *l.* 7. *p.* 47. *l.* 10.   *(o) Page* 70. *l.* 12, *and ult.*
p. 71. *l.* 2, 7 *and* 10.   *(p) Page* 74. *l.* 2 *and* 4.   *(q) Page*
5. *l.* 6. *p.* 32. *l.* 3. *p.* 44. *l.* 15. *p.* 69. *l.* 11 *and* 17. *p.* 73. *l.* 2,
and p. 74. *l.* 15.

the

the fatal Cord, as rather to be chosen than some
temporal Misfortunes, and at last resolves to die
(*r*) more like a Martyr than a Malefactor. After all this the Villain gets clear, is (*s*) the principal Hero of the Play, takes to the principal
Actress for his Wife, who shew'd her Affection in
the worst of Times, and he gives his bare Word,
that he will be constant to her, and makes an honourable Exit, without any other Sign of Repentance for, or a Reformation from his former Vil-
lanies. If then our Prisons are filled with Persons
for capital Crimes: If our Roads are infested with
Robbers abroad, and our Streets with others near-
er home: If Tradesmen cannot stir out for Fear of
being knock'd down, and their Goods cannot be
safe in their own Shops, it must be allowed, that
the Poets, Actors, and Audience have given the
greatest Encouragement to all these Misfortunes,
and have done their utmost to shock the Authority of the Laws, which are made to restrain
them, and render the Punishments inflicted in those
Cases as most contemptible.

Since therefore these *profane and vain bablings*
do (as the Text saith) *increase unto more ungodliness* ; this should exhort all such, who pretend to
a Sense of Religion, or Love to their own Souls,
to avoid them. Such *evil communications* will *corrupt good manners*, and therefore *let us not be deceived.* You cannot after such a Warning pretend to
Ignorance, and therefore the Crime must be wilful
and inexcusable. It is universally reckoned a Scandal for any Clergyman to be seen in such Places ;
and therefore that, which is scandalous in one Order, must be disreputable in others. When (*t*) St.

(*r*) *Page* 70. *l.* 17, *and p.* 71. *l.* 7.　(*s*) *Page* 75, *Scene the*
last.　(*t*) Eusebii *Historia Ecclesiastica, lib.* 3. *cap.* 28. *alias* 25.

D　　　　　　　　　　　　*John,*

John the Apoftle faw *Cerinthus* the Heretick in the fame Bath with him, he immediately withdrew himfelf, and advifed others fo to do, left the Judgments of GOD fhould overtake them for being in fuch Company ; and certainly we have as much Reafon to take his Advice, in Relation to the *Play-Houfe.* What *Tertullus* falfly faid of (*u*) St. *Paul,* is too true of fuch Actors, *We have found fuch* Men to be *peftilent Fellows,* λοιμὸν, *a Plague* ; and therefore we fhould do by them, as we do by others, who are afflicted with fuch a Diftemper. Now if we are afraid of a Difeafe, which will only kill the Body ; how much more fhould we fear that Contagion, which, if not prevented, will *deftroy both body and foul in hell?* Let us remember the Charge, which GOD gives us in the Text, and not only there, but alfo in other Places of *Scripture.* Thus it is *Eph.* v. 11, 12. *Have no fellowfhip with the unfruitful works of darknefs, but rather reprove-them* ; *For it is a fhame even to fpeak of thofe things, which are done of them in fecret.* So *Prov.* xiv. 14. &c. *Enter not into the path of the wicked, and go not in the way of evil men. Avoid it, pafs not by it, turn from it, and pafs away* ; *For they fleep not, except they have done mifchief* ; *and their fleep is taken away, except they caufe fome to fall. For they eat the bread of violence, and drink the wine of deceit.* And *Pfalm.* i. 1, 2. *Bleffed is the man, that hath not walked in the counfel of the ungodly, nor ftood in the way of finners, and hath not fate in the feat of the fcornful. But his delight is in the law of the* LORD, *and in his law will he meditate both day and night.* If thefe Places were not frequented, they would fall of courfe ; and, when the Hope of their Gains was

(*a*) Acts xxiv. 5.

gone,

gone, they might betake themselves to some reputable Method for a Livelihood. However, if some Men should be so obstinate and refractory, as to take no wholesome Advice in this Case; yet, one would think, that such *Women*, who have any Regard to their Reputation, will shun those Places. One would think, that such filthy Discourse, would be very affronting in Conversation, and not to be endured by any young *Lady*, who values her Credit. And one would think it strange, that such Liberties, which they would justly resent in private Conversation, should entertain and please them on the publick Stage. In short, their Going thither seems to be no other than Spending their Money to hear themselves abused, and their Modesty affronted; and in such a Case it is much better to stay at Home. To suppose that such can like it, is a gross Reflection on their Virtue; and therefore it may rather be hoped, that they will take Care not to expose themselves. To sit contentedly and hear a Parcel of such lewd, wanton, and smutty Discourse, both in Prose and Verse: To see such Plots and Contrivances carried on both for Whoredom and Adultery without Detestation, makes the Rakes of the Town think, that these are as bad as themselves, and that it is not a Sense of the Sin, but rather of some temporal Inconveniencies, or Want of Opportunity, which restrains them from Committing the like. This exposeth them to such Addresses, which they themselves abhor; and then, being afraid wherever they go, they wish too late, that they had never given the Occasion.

Lastly, Let us all be exhorted to put up our Prayers to GOD, *First*, For those who frequent such Places, that they may see their Error, repent of their Sin and Folly, and do so no more. If

neither

neither Sermons nor Advice can prevail; yet we know not but our Prayers may reach them, and GOD may have Mercy on them for our Sakes. *Secondly*, Let us pray to GOD for the whole Nation, that he would not lay these Sins to our Charge, but try and spare us a little longer. Never was there a greater Occasion for this than now. Do we think that there is a GOD? and that he is the Creator and Governor of the World and all that is therein? Can we (*x*) think that he will be always thus mocked, insulted, and provoked? that he will suffer his (*y*) *glory to be given to another*, and his *Praise* to the *Devil*, his greatest Enemy? and that he will not, at last, shew his Resentment and Indignation? The Prophet *Jeremiah* saith, (*z*) that when such *wonderful and horrible things* are *committed in the land, and* the *people love to have it so*, then GOD exert his Authority. *Shall I not visit for these things, saith the* LORD? *And shall not my soul be avenged on such a nation as this?* And St. *Paul* adds, (*a*) that when Men *know the judgments of* GOD, *that they who commit such things*, as Witchcraft and diabolical Representations, *are worthy of death, they have pleasure in those that do them*, they are most inexcusable. They *despise the riches of the goodness, and forbearance, and long suffering of* GOD, *not knowing that* his *goodness should lead them to repentance*. And *after* their *hardness and impenitent heart, they treasure up to themselves wrath against the day of wrath, and revelation of the righteous judgments of* GOD, *who will render to every man according to his deeds*. These old Distempers are more difficultly

(x) Gal. vi. 7.   *(y)* Isai. xlii. 8.   *(z)* Jer. vi. 29, 30, 31.   *(a)* Rom. i. 32, *and* ii. 1 *to* 12.

cured;

cured ; and therefore we may dread, that *(b)* the
Medicine of his Wrath will be more severe at laſt.
Let us then pray to him, that if the crying Sins
of this Nation are too great to be winked at, and
his Patience is provoked to Fury, yet he would at
leaſt ſpare thoſe who are innocent, and keep themſelves pure from the Pollutions of the Age ; that
he would hide them, in particular, under the Hol-
low of his Hand, until his Indignation is over-
paſt ; that he would make a *(c)* Diſtinction *between the righteous and the wicked, between him that
ſerveth* GOD, *and him that ſerveth him not* ;, that
he would *(d) ſet a mark upon the foreheads of
them that ſigh, and that cry for all the abominations, which are done in the midſt* of the Land. That
if he deals with us as with *Sodom,* for thoſe Sins in
which we imitate them ; yet that every juſt
Lot, who is grieved to hear of ſuch Things, may
be *(e)* preſerved from the Flames. That if
he ſhould ſay, *(f) Sword,* go *through the land, to
cut off from it man and beaſt,* and *make it deſolate* ;
or if he ſhould *cauſe noiſome Beaſts to paſs through*
it, or viſit us according to his daily Threatenings
with the *Famine* or the *Peſtilence* ; yet ſuch Men
as *Noah, Daniel,* and *Job,* who are found in it,
may *deliver their own ſouls by their righteouſneſs.*
And that whenever he is pleaſed again to viſit us
in Mercy, to *lift up the light of his countenance upon
us, and give us peace* ; the Senſe hereof may work
ſuch a Reformation in our Hearts, that we may no
longer be guilty of ſuch Provocations, but we
may devote ourſelves to his Service, like ſuch as

(b)   Ad pœnam tardus Deus eſt, ad præmia velox ;
      Sed penſare ſolet vi graviore moras.

(c) Mal. iii 17, 18.   *(d)* Ezek. ix. 4, 5, 6.   *(e)* 2 Pet. ii.
6, 7, 8, 9.   *(f)* Ezek. xiv. 12 *to* 21.

are

are preserved by him. To conclude, Let us all pray to GOD to give us his Grace, that we may *shun* these *profane and vain bablings*, since we find by daily and woful Experience, that *they* do *increase unto more* and more *ungodliness*. That we may delight ourselves in his Commandments, and say with holy *David*, (g) *I hate vain thoughts*, or them that imagine evil Things ; *but thy law do I love.* That instead of these profane, wanton, and ungodly Songs and Ballads, which are daily coined in this Mint of Iniquity, and tend only to the Nourishing of Vice and Corrupting of Youth, we may refresh our Souls with such *Psalms*, divine *Hymns* and *Anthems*, and such heavenly *Hallelujahs*, which an Angel may sing, or a Martyr may hear ; and which will be so far from Leaving a Sting of Conscience behind, that we may repeat them with Satisfaction on a Dying-Bed. Such *Musick* as this would revive our Souls in the greatest Affliction ; and, whilst we taste of such Enjoyments in this World, they will be but as Earnests of far greater, which we shall enjoy in the World to come.

(g) Psal. cxix. 113.

APPENDIX

APPENDIX.

Suppose that it will be urged, in Vindication of the Stage, that some of the Plays here mention'd are of an ancient Date, and are now out of Use.

To this it may be answered, that if this is true, yet it cannot be expected, that every Clergyman, who attacks the Profaneness and Lewdness of the *Play-House*, must have read the Stage quite through, or can be Judge, what are acted there, and what are not. The Reading of one or two, which are most frequented, will give a Man a Surfeit, who hath any Sense of *Religion*, and by these he may easily guess at the rest. However, this Objection is of no Force. *First*, Because they take the oldest Plays, which are fittest for their Purpose. Thus the Tragedy of *Mackbeth* continues in Esteem ; and no visible Reason can be given for it, but because the Pleasures of Witchcraft are set forth to the greatest Advantage, and herein we have a full Account of the infallible Fore-knowledge of the Devil. *Secondly,* Those Plays, *(a)* which were justly exposed by *Collier*, at the first Attack upon the *Stage*, as most scandalous for Swearing,

(a) Love for Love, and Tunbridge-Walks, &c.

Cursing,

Curfing, Smut, Burlefquing the facred *Scriptures*, and all other Sorts of Profanenefs, continue ftill to be acted with the fame Applaufe as formerly. To this may be added, that a Book was printed in the Year 1706, intituled, *The Evil and Danger of Stage-Plays, fhewing their natural Tendency to deftroy Religion, and introduce a general Corruption of Manners, in almoft two thoufand Inftances, taken from the Plays of the two former Years, againft all the Methods lately ufed for their Reformation*; and fince this another was printed in the Year 1719, intituled, *A Serious Remonftrance·in Behalf of the* Chriftian *Religion, againft the horrid Blafphemies and Impieties, which are ftill ufed in the* Englifh *Play-Houfes, to the great Difhonour of Almighty* GOD, *and in Contempt of the Statutes of this Realm, fhewing their plain Tendency to overthrow all Piety, and advance the Intereft and Honour of the Devil in the World*; *from almoft feven thoufand Inftances, taken out of the Plays of the prefent Century, and efpecially of the five laft Years, in Defiance of all Methods hitherto ufed for their Reformation.* Among others there are thefe *Chapters*, wherein the Contents are fully proved.

CHAP. 2. *The Name of the Devil is frequently mentioned on the Stage, where Men are alfo turned into Devils, and crowned with Succefs.*

CHAP. 3. *Witchcraft and Magick encouraged by the Stage.*

CHAP. 4. *The Devil honoured by the profane Swearing of the Stage.*

CHAP. 5. *The Devil honoured by the profane Curfing of the Stage.*

CHAP. 6. *Reprefentations of divine Worfhip as paid to the Devil on the Stage.*

CHAP. 7. *The Divine Attributes*, particularly his Eternity, Glory, Omniprefence, Wifdom, Knowledge,

ledge, Power, Goodnefs, Truth and Vengeance, *aſcribed to the Devil on the Stage.*

CHAP. 8. *The Scriptures perverted to the Honour of the Devil.*

CHAP. 9. *Religion, Virtue, and the Worſhip of* GOD *vilified on the Stage.*

CHAP. 10. *The Liturgy and the Articles of the* Chriſtian *Faith burleſqued by the Stage.*

CHAP. 11. *Virtue expoſed by the Stage.*

CHAP. 12. *Atheiſm and Profanenefs promoted by the Stage.*

CHAP. 13. *Vice encouraged by the Stage.*

CHAP. 14. *The Stage a declared Enemy to all Reformation.*

CHAP. 15. *Heaven, the Abode of* GOD, *expoſed on the Stage.*

CHAP. 16. *Hell, the Priſon of the Devils, magnified on the Stage.*

CHAP. 17. *Other Ways, whereby the Devil is alſo honoured, and his Intereſt directly promoted by the Stage.*

CHAP. 18. *The Bleſſed* GOD *treated with Contempt upon the Stage.*

CHAP. 19. *The Works of Creation and Providence expoſed upon the Stage.*

CHAP. 20. *The Holy Scriptures burleſqued by the Stage.*

Neither of theſe Books have yet been anſwered, neither hath there been any Method taken for their Reformation. They wholly act as their Intereſt guides them, without any Reſtraint; and we too plainly ſee, that their Intereſt guides them to pick out the worſt Plays, which were ever acted in all Ages and Places. So that whatever hath been written upon this Subject, and any Quotation from any of their Plays, is of full Force at this

E   Time,

Time, and may be alledged againſt their preſent
Practice.

Secondly, It is urged in their Vindication, That
they are obliged to make profane Perſons ſpeak
and act according to their Character. To this it
may be anſwered, That this Liberty may be allowed in every thing, which is not ſinful in it-ſelf, but
no further. But this hath been formerly and effectually anſwered. *Collier* having expoſed ſome
Plays of *Congreve* for this Reaſon, he makes this
Excuſe in print, and urged it as far as it would
go; to which *Collier* made a Reply, and ſhewed
the Weakneſs and Inſufficiency of this' Pretence.
So that they, who urge this Argument, ought
firſt to anſwer that Book, or otherwiſe it ſtands as
an Anſwer, to all that they ſtill aſſert. But the
ſtill Inſiſting on this baffled Argument ſhews
that ſuch Men will never take an Anſwer, and
with them there is no arguing. However, nothing
of this can excuſe the preſent Stage. All theſe
horrid Blaſphemies and the vileſt Expreſſions are
put into the Mouths of their principal Actors,
whom they reward at laſt, and crown with Suc-
ceſs. And this is the utmoſt, which can be done by
them to promote it in the World.

In ſhort, Profaneneſs, though never ſo well
corrected, *(b)* is not to be endured. It ought to
be baniſhed without Proviſo or Limitation. No
Pretence of Character or Puniſhment can excuſe
it, or any Stage-Diſcipline make it tolerable.
It is grating to *Chriſtian* Ears, diſhonourable to
the Majeſty of GOD, and dangerous in the Example. And it tends to no Point, unleſs it is to
wear off the Horror of the Practice, to weaken
the Force of Conſcience, and to teach the Lan-

(b) Collier's *Short View of the Stage, Page* 96.

guage

guage of the Damned. When fuch Actors are made to profper according to their Wifhes, it is much more fcandalous and provoking, and there is hardly any thing, which can exceed it, except the Pleading for it.

Laftly, It may be urged in Vindication of the *Tragedy* of *Mackbeth,* that the Confulting with Witches is difcouraged, becaufe *Mackbeth* himfelf, the principal Perfon in the Play, came to an untimely End by Confulting with them.

But to this it may be anfwered, *Firft,* That granting this to be true, yet there is no Difcouragement of *Witchcraft* or *Magick.* The *Witches* act their Parts *(c)* at feveral Times, and *(d)* make both their Entrance and their *Exit* by flying. They *(e)* fing, they *(f)* dance, they *(g)* commend their Way of Living, and feem to have nothing to difturb them, and their Character is *(h)* that *they have more in them than mortal Knowledge.*

But *Secondly,* It is not true, that Confulting with *Witches* is here difcouraged: For *Mackbeth* is not the only Inftance in this Cafe. *Banquo* had his Fortune told him, that he fhould be *(i) lefs than* Mackbeth *and greater,* and that he fhould be *(k) not fo happy, yet much happier.* The firft Part of thefe Prophecies was true in himfelf, and the other Part in his Pofterity. He was alfo told, that *(l) he fhould get Kings, but he fhould never be one.* Accordingly he was *(m)* killed when his

(c) Mackbeth, *Page* 1. *Line* 1. *p.* 3. *l.* 22. *p.* 24. *l.* 32. *p.* 39. *l.* 19, *and p.* 41. *l.* 1.　*(d)* *Page* 3. *Line* 22, *and p.* 1. *l.* 14. *(e)* *Page* 24. *Line* 32. *p.* 25. *l.* 18. *p.* 39. *l. antepenult. p.* 40. *l.* 1 *and* 23; *and p.* 42. *l.* 8.　*(f)* *Page* 26. *Line* 5.　*(g) Page* 40. *Line* 23.　*(h) Page* 10. *Line* 27.　*(i) Page* 5. *Line* 10. *(k) Page* 5. *Line* 11.　*(l) Page* 5. *Line* 12.　*(m) Page* 33. *Line* 35.

　　　　　　　　Son

Son *Flean* efcaped, and *(n) eight Kings* are fuppo-
fed to be of his Race.

Mackduff alfo confults the Witches, and had
thefe Anfwers *(o):*

1. *Saving thy Blood will caufe it to be fhed.*
2. *He'll bleed by thee, by whom thou firft haft
bled.*
5. *Thy Wife fhall fhunning Dangers Dangers
find,
And fatal be, to whom fhe moft is kind.*

The firft and third of thefe were fulfilled, becaufe upon the Death of *Banquo (p) Mackduff* flees
for *England* ; his Lady, being afraid to travel,
ftays behind ; keeps *(q)* herfelf and her Children
in a ftrong Caftle, where they were barbaroufly
murdered by *Mackbeth's* Orders. The other *(r)*
was fulfilled, when *Mackduff* killed *Mackbeth*,
faying, *I have a Prophecy, which tells me, I fhall
have his Blood, who firft fhed mine.*

Neither doth the Story of *Mackbeth* any way
difcourage the Confulting with *Witches.* They
tell him, that he was *(s) Thane* or Earl of *Gla-
mis.* This *(t)* he knew. That he was *(u) Thane*
of *Cawdor.* This *(x)* was true, but he did not
then know it. And they tell him, *(y)* that he
fhould be a King, which *(z)* happened accordingly. When they were willing to deceive him to
his own Deftruction, they tell him three Prophecies to make him bold.

(n) Page 43. *Line* 34.　　*(o) Page* 26. *Line* 11.　　*(p) Page*
37. *Line* 19.　　*(q) Page* 51. *Line* 20.　　*(r) Page* 59. *Line*
22.　　*(s) Page* 4. *Line* 34.　　*(t) Page* 5. *Line* 18.　　*(u) Page*
4. *Line* 35.　　*(x) Page* 6. *Line* 11.　　*(y) Page* 4. *Line* 36.
(z) Page 23. *Line* 26, *and p.* 26. *l.* 28.

The

APPENDIX. 37

The firſt is (*a*)

Beware Mackduff,
Avoiding him, Mackbeth *is ſafe enough.*

This was true, for (*b*) *Mackduff* killed him.

The ſecond is (*c*)

Be bold and bloody, and Man's Hatred-ſcorn;
Thou ſhalt be hurt by none of Woman born.

To which *Mackduff* (*d*) anſwers, that he

Was from his Mother's Womb untimely ript.

The laſt is (*e*)

Mackbeth *ſhall like a lucky Monarch reign,*
'Till Birnam-Wood *remove to* Dunſinain.

And accordingly (*f*) the Soldiers carried Boughs
before them to conceal their Number.

And certainly, when the *Poets* make every Tit-
tle thus fulfilled, they cannot do more to encourage thoſe *diabolical Conſultations.* But if *Mackbeth* was deſtroyed for Conſulting *Witches*, it will
alſo be remember'd, that he gained a Kingdom
by the ſame Method, and this is a ſufficient Encouragement. If the Apprehenſions of temporal
Death will not freighten Men from capital Crimes
in other Caſes, then certainly it will not in ſuch
Caſes as theſe. Beſides, Men are willing to ob-

(*a*) *Page* 43. *Line* 6.　(*b*) *Page* 59. *Line* 25.　(*c*) *Page*
43. *Line* 9.　(*d*) *Page* 59. *Line* 25.　(*e*) *Page* 43. *Line*
17. (*f*) *Page* 55. *Line* 34. *p.* 57. *l.* 16 *and* 28; *and p.* 59. *l.* 35.

tain

tain their ambitious Ends, and either look not on
such distant Consequences, or think to prevent
them by being fore-warned. If *Mackbeth*'s Example signifies any thing, the Moral is this. A
Man may gain a Kingdom by Consulting with
Witches ; but he is in Danger afterward of Coming
to an untimely End. But left this should be a
Discouragement, the *Poet* takes Care to revive the
Spirits of those, who might be afraid, and boldly
tells the Audience, (g) That

> *Those who expect, and do not fear their Dooms,*
> *May hear a Message, tho' from Hell it comes.*

The Prophet *Isaiah* tells us, that (h) his *former*
Prophecies *are come to pass* ; he also *declares new*
Things, and *tells* us *of them before they spring forth* ;
and (i) he challengeth all the Heathen Idols to
shew the things, that are to come hereafter, that we
may know them to be *gods*. The *Stage* roundly answers to this Challenge, and ascribes it all to the (k)
more than mortal or infallible Fore-knowledge of
the *Devil*, and so make his Delusions, uttered by
Witches, to vie with those sacred Oracles, formerly revealed to the Prophets.

I have dwelt the longer on this *Play*, as being
one most frequently acted. There are a vast Number of others, which are more flagrant than this.
However it is plain, that a single Sentence is often catch'd at, and turn'd to excuse the *Poet*,
when the whole Plot and Contrivance lies the contrary Way. But, alas ! the Antidote is too weak
for the Poison, or rather in this Case is no

(g) *Page* 31. *Line* 34. (h) Isaiah xlii. 9 ; *and* xliv. 24 *to the*
End. (i) Isaiah xli. 26 ; *and* xliii. 8, 9 ; *and* xliv. 7, *and* xlv. 20,
21. (k) Mackbeth, *Page* 10. *Line* 27.

Antidote

Antidote at all. It ferves only to lull the Confcience afleep, or gild the Pill, that the Poifon may be fwallowed without being fufpected.

However, as from this Inftance it is eafy to guefs at the reft; fo this may lead us into the ufual Methods of the *Stage-Poets.* They reprefent the worft Vices in the beft Drefs, and fometimes make a feint Reprefentation to the contrary, as fufficient to atone for all their Enormities. With this they endeavour to amufe the World, that Men may not think them fo bad, as they really are. Thus they ufually anfwer the Objections, which are brought againft them; and when they drown the World with an overflowing Sea of Profanenefs, they would fain make us believe, that they are inoffenfive.

An Advertifement in the *Gazette* of *October* 14, 1729.

Whitechappel Court-Houfe, Oct. 7, 1729.

Tower-Divifion.

WHereas it was publifh'd in the *Coffee-Houfe Morning Poft,* of the 24th of *September* laft, that a Gentleman, well skilled in the Management of a Theater, is obtaining Letters Patents to erect one in *Ayliffe-Street* in *Goodmans-Fields,* by Way of Subfcription, and that the Undertaking meets with a general Approbation. And alfo by an Advertifement publifhed in the *Daily Poft* of the 30th of the fame Month, it appears that only feven or eight Perfons have applied to the Juftices againft Erecting the faid Theater, but that there has been no Meeting about it. Thefe are therefore to certify, that
the

' the Erecting the said Theater is so far from
' meeting with a general Approbation, that great
' Numbers of Gentlemen and substantial Mer-
' chants and Tradesmen, residing in and near the
' said Street, have applied to His Majesty's Justi-
' ces of the Peace, acting for the Division of the
' *Tower*, at several Meetings appointed for that
' Purpose, and set forth to them the evil Conse-
' quences that will necessarily attend the Carrying
' on such a Design. The Justices present at those
' Meetings were so thoroughly convinced, that the
' Erecting the said Theater so near several publick
' Offices, and the *Thames*, where so much Busi-
' ness is negociated, and carried on for the Sup-
' port of Trade and Navigation, will draw away
' Tradesmens Servants and others from their law-
' ful Callings, and corrupt their Manners, and
' also occasion great Numbers of loose, idle, and
' disorderly Persons, as Street-Robbers, and com-
' mon Night-Walkers, so to infest the Streets, that
' it will be very dangerous for His Majesty's Sub-
' jects to pass the same, have already ordered Ca-
' veats to be enter'd in the proper Offices, to pre-
' vent the Gentlemen obtaining Letters Patents for
' Erecting the said Theater, and are resolved to the
' utmost of their Power, to shew their Disap-
' probation of the same, by doing every lawful
' Act they can, to prevent so great a Mischief.

Sign'd by Order,

Sam. Cowper, ⎫ Clerks to the Justices of the Peace,
     and   ⎬ at their Special and Petty Sessions
Sam. Sadleir, ⎭ held for the said Division.

F I N I S